Sustainable Tourism

S.P. Singh

ABD PUBLISHERS
Jaipur ■ New Delhi

Preface

The environmental quality of a tourism destination is a key factor in making decisions regarding development of tourism. Over the last decade a number of schemes have been developed worldwide to raise environmental awareness and standards of behaviour in relation to tourism. There is some evidence that a growing segment of visitors turn away from what they consider to be polluted destinations. This is specially true where health risks from air or water pollution are perceived as a problem. Environmental responsibility and environmental knowledge are two main elements through which blue flag campaign is striving for development of environmentally friendly beaches and marinas to provide clean and safe beaches and marinas for tourists and local residents. Through environmental awareness, campaign has succeeded in the improvement of coastal environment.

Tourism can provide and incentive for cleaning up the over all environment through control of water littering and through maintenance. Being largest industry in the world, tourism has the potential to become a key contributor to the preservation of natural landscapes, social structures, biodiversity, through adoption and regeneration of economically depleted areas and development of parks. Under such a preservation and conservation context the field of sustainable tourism has grown. Physical and cultural characteristics of the destinations must be taken into account as sustainable tourism respects and preferably enhances the environmental and socio-cultural carrying capacity of a destination.

"Sustainable Tourism" brings to the fore issues concerning environmental awareness and sustainability along with their impact on tourism industry worldwide. Through case studies the book makes elaborate presentation on sustainability in tourism concerning PAN parks, Mekong tourism, Coastal tourism in UK, Whistler tourism resort, tourism development plan in BINP, Uganda, convicts and conservation in Con Dao National Park, Penguins and tourists in Philip Island Nature Park, Maho Bay Resorts, Fairmont Chateau, Whistler Resort and Earth sanctuaries.

S.P. Singh

1

A Programme for Raising Environmental Awareness

Over the last decade a number of schemes have been developed to raise environmental awareness and standards of behaviour in relation to tourism. This case study provide an overview of how one such scheme, the Blue Flag campaign for beaches in Slovenia, operates. The process of creating environmental awareness through this scheme is discussed and the key elements of a successful Blue Flag campaign are identified with the aid of an environmental responsibility model. Attention is also paid to the link between the Blue Flag campaign and the growth of environmental awareness in Slovenia's tourism industry, where the campaign is seen as both a tool for improving environmental quality and a means of promoting safe beaches. However, as the Blue Flag criteria become more demanding, a development welcomed by those concerned with integrated coastal management, there is potential for conflict with tourism industry interests, an issue discussed in the conclusion to this case study.

Development of the Blue Flag Campaign

The environmental quality of a destination is a key factor in making travel-related decisions. There is some evidence that a growing segment of visitors turn away from what they consider to be polluted destinations, with tourists not willing to trade lower environmental quality for a lower price. This is especially true where health risks from air or water pollution are perceived as a problem, as illustrated by the decline in western Mediterranean tourism in the early 1990s.

The Blue Flag logo, a white circle with a bottle floating on three wave crests, is a symbol used to denote a beach or marina that has met specific environmental criteria, and as such is meant to convey a message of personal health and safety to those using them. It originated in a pollution-tracking campaign of the Foundation for Environmental Education in Europe (FEEE). This campaign involved the use of bottles containing messages total requested those finding them to contact FEEE, and was designed to track the spread of solid waste at sea. The Blue Flag programme was first launched in France in 1995, and was, at that time, concerned only with the water quality of beaches. In that year, eleven French municipalities were awarded the Blue Flag for their bathing water quality and wastewater treatment. By 1986 that number had risen to forty-three. The following year the campaign broadened to encompass a further nine countries, as well as marinas, as an activity of the European Year of the Environment Co-ordination of this expanded programme fell to FEEE and the Commission of the European Communities. In subsequent years the Blue Flag campaign continued to grow, under the umbrella of FEEE, and with the help of its national branches in each participating country. In 2001, Blue Flags were awarded to 2,041 sea and inland water beaches and 713 marinas in 21 European countries:

Belgium	Finland	Italy	Slovenia
Bulgaria	France	Latvia	Spain
Croatia	Germany	The Netherlands	Sweden
Cyprus	Greece	Norway	Turkey
Denmark	Ireland	Portugal	United Kingdom
Estonia			

In 2001, for the first time, the campaign will travel beyond Europe to South Africa and the Caribbean. With the spreading of the campaign to non-European countries FEEE has now been renamed FEE (Foundation for Environmental Education), with the words 'in Europe' removed from its name.

The Blue Flag Campaign in Slovenia

Slovenia is a new transitional country that was established in 1991 when it separated from the former Yugoslavia. Geographically, it lies in the north-east corner of the Adriatic Sea, between the Italian and Croatian seasides, and has a 46-kilometers-long coastline with thirty-one public beaches. Tourism along this coastline is highly developed, with 1.6 million tourist nights being spent in its resort towns. This figure represents more than 25 per cent of total tourist nights in Slovenia.

In socialist Slovenia environmental issues were not high on the political agenda. Arguably, the first time concerns were raised concerning the environmental effects of tourism was at the Tourism Forum, a component of the Alpe Adria tourism fair in the capital Ljubljana in 1992. At this time, however, there appeared to be little desire on behalf of the tourism industry to address environmental quality issues. Indeed, some Forum participants were concerned that to do so could damage the image of Slovenia's coastal tourism product. Given that at the year prior to the Forum, 52 per cent of Slovenian beaches, according to government tests, did not meet national standards for bathing water quality, such a view is perhaps understandable.

After 1991 environmental awareness in Slovenia started to develop rapidly due to the increased flow of information from beyond the state's now open borders. Additionally, many foreign consultants from different fields were hired by the new democratically elected government, to advise it one various matters, including environmental management. It was in this atmosphere of change and the reappraisal of old practices and ideas, that the concept of sustainability became integrated into the national tourism development strategy. External pressures were also serving at this time to push beach tourism operators in the direction of being more environmentally aware. For example, international tour operators, especially the German tour operator Touristic Union International (TUI), checked the environmental performance of its partners and identified Blue Flag beaches and marinas in its catalogues.

In 1993 the Ministry for Industry, then responsible for tourism, spurred on, in part, by a group comprising enlightened members of the tourism industry, institutions involved in tourism research, and several journalists with an interest in the environment, asked the

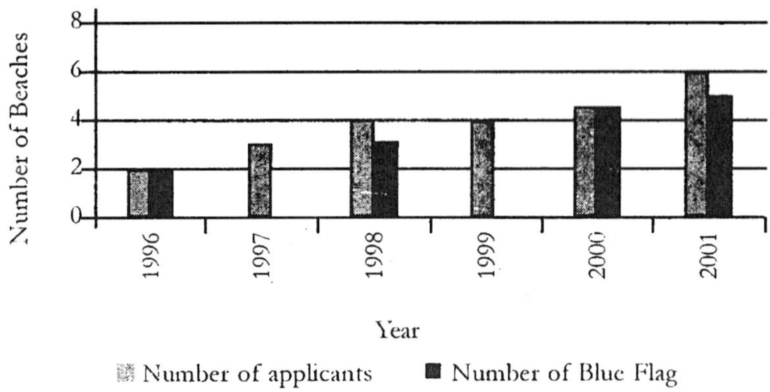

Figure 1. Numbers of applicant and awarded Blue Flag beaches in Slovenia 1996–2001.

Faculty of Economics at the University of Ljubljana to establish contact with the international Blue Flag authorities and initiate efforts to obtain the European environmental mark for Slovenian marina and beach tourism. Contact with FEEE was successfully achieved and an attempt was made to house the Blue Flag campaign within the existing National Tourism Association. FEEE foresaw the possibility of a conflict of interest with this arrangement and suggested the creation of a new non-governmental organisation with a clear general aim to increase environmental awareness through the activities of FEEE. Accordingly, the above-mentioned group of enthusiasts joined with representatives from health institutions, environmental organisations and government to set up the Foundation for Environmental Education in Europe-Slovenia (FEEE-S). This body became a member of FEEE in 1994. In the role of 'a department', the Italian national FEEE operator worked closely with the Slovenian organisation to help implement the Blue Flag campaign in Slovenia.

In Slovenia the marina Blue Flag campaign started in 1995 and the beach campaign in 1996. In 1996 two beach applicants met all the standards and were awarded the blue logo; by 2001 this number had climbed to six (Figure 1). Over this same period (Figure 1), a number of beaches were also rejected. Indeed, in 1997 and 1999 when no Slovenian beach was successful in gaining a Blue Flag award, media and public debate on water quality and broader issues relating to tourism and environmental quality increased dramatically.

Blue Flag Award Criteria

Criteria for being awarded a Blue Flag are pre-defined by the FEEE Blue Flag campaign and are merely implemented by each national operator. For the 2001 bathing season there were twenty-seven criteria for beaches that related to four key aspects. Some of the criteria relating to each of these four areas are given here for illustrative purposes.

- *Water quality*. The criteria here state that there must be compliance with requirements and standards such as those of the EU's Bathing Water Directive. This directive prescribes the percentage of test results that must comply with guideline and imperative values for total and faecal colibacteria and faecal streptococci. There are also standards on colour, transparency, mineral oils, phenols content and other substances. Furthermore, no sewage discharges may affect the beach area, and the community must observe sewage treatment requirements of the EU's Urban Waste Water Directive. This directive sets exact standards for treatment and discharged of urban wastewater and requires that all the sewage discharged must be collected and treated. It sets different standards and implementation deadlines according to the type of area and size of the settlement.

- *Environmental education and information.* Information in flora and fauna must be publicly displayed, including advice on how to behave, to minimise impacts on these. Data on bathing water quality also needs to be displayed on the beach in the form of a table of figure that can be easily understood.
- *Environmental management and facilities.* Example criteria are: rubbish bins in adequate numbers that are properly secured and regularly maintained and emptied; safe access paths to the beach; facilities for receiving recyclable materials; the presence of local land-use and development plans for the coastal zone; and the active promotion of sustainable transport to and along the beach area (*i.e.*, bicycling, walking or public transport).
- *Safety and services.* Requirements relate to such matters as: the presence of beach guards; first aid service provision of drinking water, access and facilities for people with disabilities; and general maintenance of buildings and equipment.

Some Blue Flag criteria are imperatives, like the water quality criteria or litter bins in adequate numbers, while others are merely guidelines, such as recycling waste materials. A beach that does not comply with one or more of the imperative criteria cannot be awarded a Blue Flag. Each year a number of guideline criteria become imperative and new criteria may be added. The same criteria apply for candidates from all states. Where national legislation is stricter on a particular issue, this must be complied with rather than the Blue Flag criterion. For example, the Slovenian national standards on bathing water quality are stricter than those of the EU, which form the basis of the Blue Flag standards.

At the moment the Blue Flag beach campaign relates to operated urban beaches. The beach operator (who is licensed by local government) can act directly to fulfil some criteria (*e.g.*, provision of beach access for people with disabilities), whereas the fulfilment of others (*e.g.*, the new EU Urban Waste Water Directive), may call for the engagement of the local community and other partners, even the national government.

Partners in the Blue Flag Campaign

The Blue Flag campaign works at three levels: local, national and international.

Local level

At the local level, the Slovenian campaign involves direct and indirect partners. According to the application procedure, direct partners are the beach operator and the local government. The beach operator makes the initial decisions to apply for a Blue Flag, and application in then made on its behalf by the local government to the Slovenian national Blue Flag organisation (FEEE-S). The involvement of local authorities is necessary since they have many responsibilities regarding the Blue Flag criteria. These include waste-water treatment, organising the collection of rubbish, ensuring visitor safety on beaches and incorporating environmental considerations into local planning. Additionally, the local community must have a land-use and development plan for its coastal zone. This plan, and the current activities of the community in the coastal zone, must be in compliance with planning regulations and coastal zone protection regulations. Although such criteria are of no direct value to beach visitors, they generally push tourism development in the local community in a more environmentally friendly direction. Directly they do not communicate the message on environmental quality, but in the long run they contribute to it.

The beach operator in Slovenia works with the Blue Flag co-ordinator from the national organisation in order to ensure that all criteria that are the responsibility of the beach operator are met. Amongst others, the authorised beach operator or beach owner is responsible for drinking water sources on the beach, toilets, rubbish collection, displaying the relevant criteria, informing beach visitors on environmental matters concerning their use of the area, and obtaining and displaying regular water quality results in a form that can be easily understood.

At the local level, many other indirect participants are involved in the Blue Flag campaign. Organisations, such as local associations, local businesses and tourist associations have an interest in obtaining the Blue Flag for a local beach. They may also have interests that are in line with the aims of the campaign and therefore they might act to co-operate in Blue Flag activities within their local community or with the national organisation itself. As regards this last point, the Slovenian Blue Flag campaign has relationships with the Sanitary Microbiological Laboratory, conservation organisations, environ-mental organisations, the Institute for Protection of the Natural Environment and Cultural Heritage, as well as with other partners in the coastal community. Also, the local population has a vested interest in the success of the campaign, and it is therefore in their interests to support it in whatever ways they can.

National level

The Blue Flag campaign within Slovenia is co-ordinated at the national level by the FEEE-S (Foundation for Environmental Education of Europe in Slovenia). This body is a voluntary, independent, non-profit, and non-governmental association. Its main aim is to raise environmental awareness in Slovenia. It acts to inform the public regarding matters associated with environmental protection; it organises and manages various activities of the international organisation FEE, of which it is a full member, and also represents Slovenia within this organisation.

The FEEE-S, as the national Blue Flag co-ordinator, works with local communities and other parties interested in applying for Blue Flags. At the same time, it represents the Blue Flag campaign's interests *vis-à-vis* national authorities such as the Ministry for the Environment and Regional Planning, and Health Ministry for Sport, Science and Education.

The Slovenian international jury meets once a year and selects applicants who are then sent before the International Jury of FEE.

International level

As of 2001 the Blue Flag scheme involved twenty-one European and one non-European country (South Africa), which work under the international umbrella organisation known as FEE (Foundation for Environmental Education).

FEE's primary role is to promote environmental education, and in doing this it offers its members four general environmental-awareness raising projects: Eco Schools, Young Reporters for the Environment, Learning about Forests and the Blue Flag Campaign (FEE, 2001). These programmes are delivered/conducted through a network of national operators under common standards and criteria. FEE's headquarters are presently in England, and decisions regarding its activities and policies, etc., are made by its annual general assembly.

The Blue Flag, as one of the FEE's campaigns, is run through the European Blue Flag secretariat in Copenhagen. Its activities include: organising meetings for national operators to discuss common problems and future changes to Blue Flag criteria; facilitating the exchange of information and expertise among countries; the production of common European information and promotional materials; and the running of the European Jury.

Contribution to Environmental Responsibility

The Blue Flag campaign for environmentally responsible beaches and marinas started out as a way of encouraging local authorities to provide clean and safe beaches and marinas for tourists and local residents. But the campaign has been increasingly conducted within the much wider context of environmental management of the coastal area, and the criteria used in the campaign have been progressively broadened. The campaign's long-term objectives are to improve environmental awareness of the coastal environment and promote environmental behaviour, thereby developing environmental responsibility.

Environmental responsibility and **environmental knowledge** are two main foundation elements that help to explain how an environmental campaign works. In the model presented in Figure 2 they are presented as the overriding essential elements. In this model environmental responsibility is connected to environmental awareness, ethics and behaviour. Environmental responsibility requires both an awareness of environmental problems and behaviour that complies with environmental ethics. Thus, environmental behaviour is only possible if environmental awareness and ethics exist.

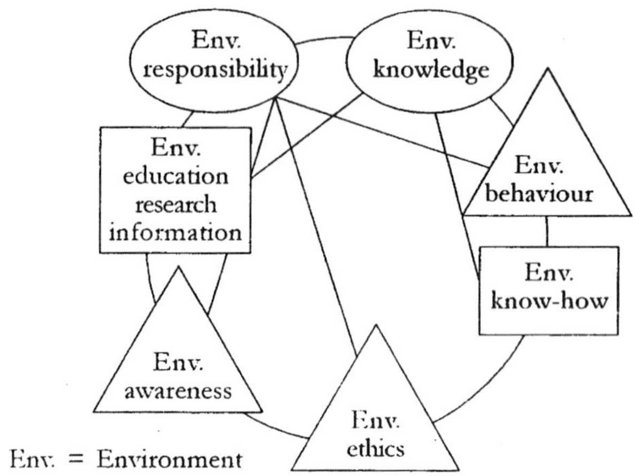

Figure 2. Know-how as an essential element of the environmental responsibility—knowledge model.

Environmental damage arising from, for example, improper behaviour may also be due to human ignorance. Human ignorance is often caused through insufficient education, research, and information. Since environmental disasters may develop over a long period, a direct link with concrete human actions may not be visible; therefore a lack of understanding and information is often the real reason why such disasters arise. If humans had sufficient information about the consequence of their actions, such disasters may not happen. This is illustrated by the second foundation element in the model, environmental knowledge. This model element consists of two parts: environmental education, research and available information on the one hand and environmental know-how on the other. The latter refers to knowledge on appropriate criteria and the means on technical, financial, managerial and organisational implementation of environmental action, such as how to carry out water testing, and how to construct purifying plants in order to meet defined standards.

The Blue Flag campaign offers pre-defined criteria for the environmentally appropriate management of beaches and local communities. In Figure 2 the environmental know-how of the Blue Flag campaign is placed between environmental ethics (what is right and what is wrong) and environmental behaviour, and is seen as a connecting elements (how to do it properly). Environmental education, research and information are presented as important elements in the creation of envioronmental awareness, which is the main aim of the Blue Flag campaign. For Slovenia, Blue Flag's environmental information potential is especially important. Amongst other things, the Blue Flag campaign informs the public about environmental quality and, at the same time, she Slovenian FEEE-S is pushing for public availability of all environmental quality seta in order to promote and speed up environmental problem-solving through public pressure.

The effectiveness of the Blue Flag campaign can be partially judge by how well it addresses the elements of this model. In that regard, Kernel examined the environmental education, awareness' and behaviour outcomes of Blue Flag From the perspectives of national tourism organisations, national Blue Flag juries, FEE member organisations and national environmental organisation in fourteen European countries. According to that survey 80 per cent of tourism organisations, 81 per cent of national FEE branch organisation and 60 per cent of environmental organisation believed that the campaign had raised environmental awareness. The results also showed that there was still a gap between awareness and environmental behaviour, with less than 30 per cent of respondents believing that the Blue Flag campaign actually changed the behaviour of visitors.

Conclusion

Tourism can provide an incentive for cleaning up the overall environment through control of water littering, and for improving environmental aesthetics through maintenance. In the Mediterranean region there is much justifiable concern being expressed about marine pollution, and hence there is a significant role for a campaign like Blue Flag. The campaign has now reached a stage where it is sufficiently established in Europe for the possession of a Blue Flag to mean something to visitors, or at least to tourism businesses. The previously mentioned survey by Kernel revealed that 24 per cent of truism organisation beloved that visitors preferred blue Flag beaches over others. Having a Blue Flag signifies a safe and clean beach with good water quality, while not having, or losing one, may raise questions about water quality in the public media.

The number of Slovenian Blue Flag beaches is still relatively low; five Blue Flag sea beaches out of a potential thirty-two, representing only 15 per cent of the total. On the other hand, all three Slovenian marinas were awarded the Blue Flag logo in 2000 and 2001. The low number of applications from Slovenian beaches is due to the very complex criteria that have to be fulfilled by the beach operator, although more are preparing to apply in the near future. Nevertheless, the Blue Flag campaign in Slovenia can be regarded as successful tool for addressing environmental problems and implementing internationally recognised standards.

Finally, it has to be emphasised that environmental impacts are not always controlled by the beach operator or tourism business. The Blue Flag is awarded on the basis of the water quality of the beach; yet the organisation responsible may not be able to control sources of pollution whose origination for example, might be located some distance away, being carried by wind and currents. Hence the decision-making processes associated with such plans. In this regard, FEEE-S in now being challenged to change Blue Flag's image so that it comes to seen as a tool for progressing interacted sustainable development in costal areas that is beneficial not only to the tourism industry, but also to local communities. According to Kernel , such an aim is in line with how environmental organisations in European countries primarily consider the Blue Flag campaign, forty-two per cent of those organisation, as opposed to less than 10 per cent of national tourism organisation exposed Blur Flag to promote interacted coastal area management and control.

2

PAN Parks: WWF's Sustainable Tourism Certification Programme

The Context and Nature to PAN Parks

Tourism is one of the largest industries in Europe, and has the potential to become a key contributor to the preservation of rural European landscapes and social structures through the regeneration of economically depleted areas. Although coastal and city tourism are still the highest in terms of visitor numbers, it is rural and mountain tourism that is showing particularly strong growth in the European context, and this is mostly around protected areas. The IUCN lists four reasons why the 1990s have offered increased opportunities for protected areas, all of which apply to Europe:

1. human populations are relatively stable and affluent;
2. there are declining pressures on land in many areas because of agricultural surpluses and reduced military activity;
3. there is a high level of public support for conservation; and
4. there is a climate if international cooperation.

Given these trends, the threat to protected areas in Europe has diminished, particularly from such activities as resource extraction and agriculture. Nonetheless, land use pressures remain evident due to limited land availability, with tourism and recreation being amongst the greatest contributors to such pressure in the context of Europe's national parks. It is also the case that the increasing use of natural areas for these purposes has generated a stronger commitment by governments and the broader community to their preservation.

There are between 10,000 and 20,000 protected areas in Europe; although the number is high, many are generally smallholdings containing pockets of biodiversity and few are large enough to allow for the free roaming of large mammals. It is also evident that the level of protection, the presence of multiple use objectives, level of funding, and state intervention/permissiveness vary significantly between these areas. In response to these, and other issues, the European Commission developed Natura 2000 as their strategy for environmental conservation. As part of this strategy, two tourism-related projects have been identified as being particularly relevant to the implementation of this strategy. The first one of these is the European Charter for Sustainable Tourism in Protected Areas, headed by the *Parcs Naturels Régionaux* de France under the auspices of the Europarc Federation, and supported by the IUCN. The Charter developed by this project has been tested in ten European national parks, and these have been acknowledged as well-managed protected areas that have made continuous efforts towards making tourism and conservation compatible. The second, and the focus of this case study, is the PAN Parks network of protected areas. PAN Parks is the result of a partnership established in 1997 between the World Wide Fund for Nature-Netherlands and the Dutch Molecaten Group, a leisure and tourism-based corporation with assets of 45 million euros and an annual turnover of 13.5 million euros, which develops holiday villages in Europe.

The concept behind PAN Parks is one of creating a network of natural areas with an international reputation for outstanding access to wildlife and excellent tourist facilities, combined with effective habitat protection and the minimal environmental impact possible. Given this goal, PAN Parks has sought to develop:

- a recognisable network of well-managed, protected natural areas which welcome visitors and avoid potentially conflicting activities;
- a partnership between the authorities of protected areas, the local population, and commercial and nature conservation organisations;
- a way to promote well managed natural areas to create a balance between nature conservation, local development, tourism and recreation; and
- an organisation to increase the number of well-supervised natural areas in Europe.

In essence, the PAN Parks project is trying to create a network of 'Yellowstone Parks' in Europe. The intention being one of identifying protected areas holding wilderness characteristics and tourist attractiveness, not only of national but also of pan-European importance, encouraging the sustainable environmental and tourism management of these areas, and promoting visitation to them. The concept of reproducing the success of American parks in tourism is an ambitious challenge for Europe. There are no more than 100 parks that would qualify on size alone. Most of these are located in Eastern Europe, where problems such as overstretched budgets, little tourism infrastructure, limited visitor management experience and where local use of parks for poaching and illegal harvesting exist. Yet the preservation of these areas in the medium term, and the link via corridors between the remaining pieces of wilderness in Europe in the long-term, could have an invaluable impact on the preservation of the regions' wildlife.

PAN Parks and the European Charter are working jointly to benefit from synergies between their projects. Cees Lager, CEO of the Molecaten Group, sees the benefits in tourism development that are linked to nature conservation, and views the inclusion of non-financial returns on investment, such as nature conservation, as a key value in this project. At the same time, however, Lager notes that for the project to be successful, acceptable financial returns must be forthcoming to those that invest in it. PAN Parks Accommodation BV is the limited liability company made up of investing partners, and initially managed by Molecaten, that will seek investors to provide 'appropriate accommodation (to be called PAN Villages) at approved PAN Parks, to generate income for its shareholders and to provide financial support for the PAN Parks Foundation.' Molecaten and other investors will 'help project and develop many of Europe's most beautiful wilderness areas while enjoying a sound return on their investment.' It is unclear at this early stage what percentage of profits will be distributed to shareholders, used for reinvestment purpose or allocated to the Foundation.

This case study discusses the process of engaging a core group of European parks in the development and implementation of habitat, visitor, tourism and business management strategies in their process of application for the PAN Parks quality trademark, and ultimately to ensure a more sustainable use of the parks' resources. The first section reviews the applicants to PAN Parks and the benefits from application as presented by the PAN Parks Foundation and perceived by the applicants. This is followed by a review of the key principles of the process of compliance assessment and how PAN Parks is following this process of setting up criteria, ensuring the criteria are assessable, verifying standards of applicants, certification of results and ensuring recognition and acceptance by the target audiences. Since PAN Parks is still in its early years, this case study focuses on the outcomes from the first stage and critically assesses the main challenges to be faced if the programme is to contribute to sustainable tourism.

The PAN Parks Candidates

For parks to qualify for inclusion in the PAN Park network they need to be large (usually over 25,000 hectares), with evidence of outstanding environmental quality and management. The candidates listed in Table 1 were present at the first Candidate PAN Parks Conference, held in Holland in June 2001. PAN Parks aims to appoint another six out of a preliminary list of ten other parks as prospective candidates in the near future.

Table 1. First Candidate Presented for PAN Parks

Name of area	*Country*	*Area (ha)*	*Visitors per year*	*Strengths*	*Weaknesses*
1	*2*	*3*	*4*	*5*	*6*
Abbruzo National Park	Itlay	43,950	2,000,000	1,600 small-scale businesses in operation. Local people represented on board of directors.	No distinct management plan document.
Bieszczady National Park	Poland	29,200	250,000	Trilateral Man and Biosphere Reserve. 70 per cent of park is strictly protected.	Park is perceived as limiting to local development.
Fulufjällets Nature Reserve	Sweden	35,000	100,000	Local people are interested in PAN Parks.	Traditional use of resources.
Mercantour National Park	France	68,500	550,000	Partnership with Gites Panda. Twinned with Italian Park.	Conflicts with shepherds on wolf issue. Local people have just started to realise importance of tourism.

1	*2*	*3*	*4*	*5*	*6*
Oulanka National Park	Finland	27,500	150,000	Park can raise income for itself. Local people are active in park management issues.	There is no co-operation with local companies. Park does not communicate with local communities.
Slovensky raj National Park	Slovak Rep.	32,774	500,000	Comparative advantage in Slovakia, well-known park. Close working relationships with PAN Parks office.	Pressure on environment from high level of visitation. Land use problems due to contradictions in zoning.
Triglav National Park	Slovenia	83,807	720,000	History of co-operation with local communities. No hunting on 25,000 hectares.	Pressure on environment from high levels of visitation. Limited co-operation between groups associated with tourism in the park.

Source: Adapted from *PAN Parks Courier*, 2001.

The parks that have so far been selected as official candidates for inclusion in the PAN Park network represent some of the richest natural resources of Europe. They are home to large mammals and predators such as wolf, chamois, bears, lynx, moose and eagle. As examples, there are 200 rare animal species in Bieszczady, 100 Marsican Brown Bears and 60 Appenine wolves in Abbruzzo, and 6,300 chamois in Mercantour. Besides their animal wealth, these parks are also sites of high concentration of species. Triglav has combined 5,500 species of flora and fauna within its boundaries. Abruzzo has one-third of the higher order plants of Italy, and Oulanka has 500 species of vascular plants, which is unusual given its northern location. Mercantour is home to 2,000 species of plants, including 60 species of orchids, 200 rare and 300 endemic species, due to landscapes ranging from Mediterranean (20 kilometres away from the sea) to Alpine (3,000 metre high mountains with glaciers). Slovensky raj has more than 2,100 species of butterflies due to its high concentration of gorges and caves.

Many of the candidate parks have a wide range of facilities: Abruzzo has 15 visitor centres and ten mountain refuges, Oulanka has 36 cooking and camp fires, 32 campsites and eight unlocked cabins for recreational use, and Triglav has 32 alpine houses and huts. Land use in these parks varies, and although they all have core conservation areas, poaching and illegal hunting are still common. Some parks, such as Triglav which generates 40 per cent if its funds from tourism and recreation, are already benefiting from visitation; however, such parks tend to be the exception rather than the rule. In general, most parks rely on government funds, with tourism benefits being captured by nearby communities. Oulanka typifies this situation, with its management noting that it gains no revenue from its 120,000 visitors, yet it is estimated that 30 per cent of the income from the neighbouring towns is attributable to tourists visiting the park.

Short- and Long-term Benefits to the Parks

The current candidates for inclusion in PAN Parks acting to pilot the processes and materials that have been developed for the project.

Each candidate park must demonstrate that it is performing at a high level in at least one area covered by the scheme, and parks are encouraged to share information in order to reach acceptable benchmarks as they seek to move from 'candidate' status to become a verified member of it.

Parks can benefit from WWF support in training and resources to meet the scheme's criteria, and once they qualify certified parks can use the PAN Parks logo for marketing purposes. Table 2 shows a list of benefits categorised according to whether a park has been verified and certified, is a candidate park aiming for verification, or has made prospective enquiries but not yet entered the process as a candidate. The benefits of working towards the PAN Parks standards are not clear to every park, and in the last three years many parks have shown interest for a short period of time, after which they have decided not to go forward. Out of the current parks working towards certification (seven), the two in France and Italy, with longer experience in tourism management, have been most critical of the benefits that can be gained from the process, whereas parks with lower tourist number have shown more interest.

The benefits that PAN Parks lists in Table 2 generally coincide with park managers' expectations of the outcomes from this process. In general, park managers view PAN Parks as a quality trademark; however, what each park seeks from the scheme is dependent on their specific circumstances. The anticipated benefits for each park include opportunities for increased, mainly international, tourism business (Fulufjället, Mercantour, Triglav, Oulanka), networking and research opportunities (Abruzzo, Bieszczady, Mercantour, Slovesky raj, Triglav), and closer co-operation with local populations and stakeholders (Oulanka, Slovensky raj).

As regards tourism benefits, when Cees Lager, from the Molecaten group, introduced the first Candidate PAN Parks Conference in 1999 he did so by highlighting the market demand for ecotourism that can be experienced in relative comfort. While the desire to service this market niche was central amongst his group's decision to support the PAN Park concept, there is no obligation on the part of participating parks to allow PAN Villages to be developed within their boundaries. At the commencement of 2002, only two candidate parks, Bieszczady and Fulufjället, had decided to proceed with proposals to develop PAN Villages. Fulufjället PAN Village, for example, is intending to include forty self-catering chalets with planning permission for a total of 62 the construction of infrastructure will be completed by summer 2002 and the chalets by 2003, with the villages to be opened on 1 July, 2004.

Table 2. PAN Park benefits to be verified, candidate and prospective candidate parks

Benefits	*Verified park*	*Candidate park*	*Prospective park*
Introduction of a PAN Park village	(√)		
Pan Parks Foundation support	√		
Access to loans	√		
Access to EU subsidies	√		
Access to on-site conservation projects	√	√	
Training material and opportunities	√	√	
Inclusion in PAN Parks brochures	√	√	
Communication package	√	√	
Local partner website	√	√	
Benefits from PAN Parks research	√	√	√
Access to the PAN Parks intranet	√	√	√
Promotion at the PAN Parks website	√	√	√
PAN Parks Courier (magazine)	√	√	√

(√) PAN Park Villages will be introduced on a longer-term basis.

Most candidate parks have stated that PAN Parks has given them a medium-term goal and a short-term pathway to put into practice a variety of actions that have been on the 'back burner' for some time. Community consultation and the development of visitor and tourism management strategies are the short-term benefits mentioned most often. Besides these general considerations, two examples can be given of the benefits of PAN Parks to prospective candidate parks to date. Firstly, PAN Parks is helping promote tourism to the Bialowieza National Park (Poland), a prospective candidate park. Secondly, Fulufjället Nature Reserve has submitted a proposal to the European Union to be reclassified as a National Park, which has been accepted and will become operational in 2002 in part due to the support of PAN Parks. To assess the possible long-term benefits of PAN Parks it is necessary to review the process that applicants will have to follow in their efforts to achieve certification.

Standards

A standard is a document approved by a recognised body that provides for common and repeated use of a prescribed set of rules, conditions, or requirement. Setting standards is one of the hardest elements of a project of this type, since varying geographical and other site specific conditions mean what is appropriate for one park may not be acceptable elsewhere. For example, slash and burn is a traditional practice in Finland that has been lost over the years, and in the Koli National Park (Finland) this practice has been reintroduced as a mean of rescuing traditions, yet forest fire is a major threat to national parks in the Mediterranean. Another major difficulty arises from differences in national legislation, practices and objectives. Ideally, standards should not be below any national legislative requirements, but if a standard reflects the highest level of current law and practice this might be too demanding for some countries. For these reasons the standards PAN Parks have developed tend to be a mixture of environmental performance and environmental management.

PAN Parks is developing its standards in the form of criteria, grouped under five principles. A manual of good practice for parks needing support to meet the requirements of these principles will be developed, which will include case studies from pilot sites.

Principles and Criteria

PAN Parks had laid out five principles for assessment of each member park's performance and management. The first three principles are under the control of the park's management unit, whereas the fourth and fifth principles are more challenging, since they recognise the dependence between the park and its surroundings, and the need for the park to engage with a variety of stakeholders in determining limits of acceptable change from tourism.

The **first principle** relates to a park's natural heritage, and acts as a filter to ensure that a park is worthy of inclusion in the PAN Parks project. The **second principle** concerns the degree of management effectiveness exhibited in the protection of the natural environment. The **third principle** relates to the park's visitor management strategy and plan, including the provision and interpretation to visitors. These first three principles could be seen as somewhat predictable given the objectives of the project, and it is therefore not surprising that they were the first agreed to. To two subsequent principles are more innovative and therefore have received more attention here.

The **fourth principle** pertains to the sustainable tourism development strategy of the park and its zone of influence, ensuring that development around the park is in keeping with the values of the area, taking into account visitor needs as well as environmental, socio-economic and cultural constraints. This is a challenging principle since the park's management has limited influence over what takes place outside its boundaries. Nonetheless, park authorities need to see beyond their physical boundaries. Since the activities taking place in neighbouring towns and villages rely in many ways on the park, and also affect the use of the park's resources.

The **fifth principle** is linked to the quality of the park's business partners. It extends principle 4 by requiring the park to set up agreements with individual companies that commit themselves to being assessed against a set of criteria, which includes demonstrating how they can support the park's objectives and contribute to their implementation. This implies that parks will have to identify and communicate potential benefits to those businesses aiming to become partners. Organisations with which partnerships may be established extend beyond those involved in the tourism industry to encompass any business or association that can prove it has a vested interest in, or influence on, a park. It is also noteworthy that any international organisation wishing to use a park will be encouraged to be certified by a relevant body or to be involved in recognisable programmes such as the Tour Operators Initiative for Sustainable Tourism Development. Partner bodies will also be encouraged to be part of a forum involved in the sustainable tourism development strategy. However, their involvement in decision-making will depend on their relationship to the area. For example, hotels, inbound tour operators and shops trading directly with tourists will have a greater say than outbound tour operators from overseas, since the former have made a long-term investment in the destination and rely on the long-term sustainable use of the park's resources, whereas the latter can easily move their business away from the area.

The principles and associated criteria noted previously were field tested in 1999. Once a basic 'shell' was agreed, indicators were introduced to verify the criteria. These were tested in a second round of consultations that involved the self-assessment of 17 national parks from 14 countries. After this consultation phase was complete the principles and criteria were further evolved with the assistance of the Societé Générals de Surveillance (SGS) Hungary; Europarc; and an independent consultant. Flowing from this process was the present set of principles and criteria.

Assessment, Verification and Certification

The process associated with assessment, verification and standardization involves following steps:

1. the park's management unit submits an assessment, which is made on the basis of the checklist (principles 1–3). Any area will be able to download the application form from the PAN Parks web page (www.panparks.org);
2. the assessment is evaluated by PAN Parks and a decision is made whether it seems to worth verifying it;

3. the park, with expert support from PAN Parks, will devise a plan to meet the requirements of the criteria, and collect evidence for each one of the indicators, by a negotiated date;
4. the verifiers travel to the area to review evidence;
5. verifiers submit their recommendation for improvements; and
6. certification is awarded/or recommendations for improvements needed to meet standards are provided to the management of the park.

The assessment process (step 2) will be guided by the use of indicators that will serve to determine a park's performance against a specific principle and its associated criteria. In table 3 an example of indicators has been given. If a park moves on to step 3 it is given the status of candidate and provided with training recourses and other benefits. Candidature periods are negotiated individually with parks depending on their current position, demonstrating the open

Table 3 Assessment Indicators Linked to Criteria

Criterion	*Indicators*
The protected area has a visitor management plan that is actively implemented. Regular monitoring and assessment of the plan are carried out and modifying the plan in light of the results of this.	• Provide the visitor management plan (an English summary and a copy, (if available). • Provide information of the plans long- and short-term goals. • Provide information on the resources available for the implementation of the visitor management plan. • Describe how the effect of the visitor management plan's actions are being monitored. • Indicate how the plan can be revised accordingly.

and flexible approach taken by PAN Parks in encouraging applications to set their own agendas. At the end of the candidature period the park will submit a report detailing their progress in meeting the five principles and their associated criteria. To assist parks in working their way through the candidature process, PAN Parks conducts workshops at which parks develop their initial draft strategies. The first of these was conducted in Holland in June 2001 and was attended by all the current (seven) candidate parks.

Once a candidature period is over, and the park concerned has submitted a report, a verification process takes place. This involves a site visit and a review of desk evidence such as plans, minutes of meetings, procedures, surveys, assessments and so on. PAN Parks has opted for third party verification, involving the contracting of independent individuals. Other approaches to the verification process were considered, but they were found to have limitations. PAN Parks staff, for example, could have been used for this purpose, but it was felt that a conflict of interest might arise from having the same staff that provided support throughout the process being asked to do the assessment. Another option was to contract an external company to undertake all verifications; however, the small scale of PAN Parks does not make this feasible. PAN Parks plans to have eight parks verified by 2006.

During a workshop held in Zwolle, the Netherlands, on 11 April, 2000, participants agreed that the PAN Parks Foundation must develop its own verification manual, which can be provided to a third party verifier in order to undertake the required field verification. With this goal in mind, Société Général de Surveillance (SGS) Hungary was appointed to develop a verification manual including general guidelines and check-lists. SGS is one of the world leaders in verification, testing and certification and has collaborated closely with Green Globe 21. Once developed, the manual will be tested and finalised through field trials in pilot areas. The manual will then be available to independent experts contracted as verifiers. The process of developing the manual and finalising the principles and criteria system, including measurable and objective indicators, was due for completion in October 2001.

Exact fees for involvement in the programme, and the associated use of the PAN Parks logo, have yet to be set. Nonetheless, fees will be subsidised by 50 per cent for European Union countries and up to 75 per cent for EU Accession countries, including Eastern Europe, where most applicants are based. The fees will be used for third-party verification and for providing other services, such as consultants or training programmes. The cost of operating PAN Parks is much higher than the fees paid by members, and the operations of the secretariat function of the PAN Parks Foundation, membership services, and publications will require external funding. Such funding will be provided by the Molecaten group in the short- to medium-term; with its longer-term capacity/willingness to do so likely to be linked to its success in establishing PAN Villages in, or once adjacent to, participating parks. A complicating factor here is that once a park is certified and a village built (optional under the scheme), if the park concerned later comes into question there is the potential for a conflict of interest to emerge between the accommodation and the certification arms. This is an issue that PAN Parks Foundation is aware of but has not yet determined how to resolve.

Recognition and Acceptance

Recognition and acceptance of the PAN Parks trademark will be driven by a communication's campaign conducted directly by the PAN Parks organisation, the parks themselves and the distributors of tourism products. This process will be costly, and as such it is one of the major drawbacks of certification systems of this kind. At present, PAN Parks are communicating with four groups: pilot PAN Parks and self-assessment participants, WWF-offices, (potential) investors and (potential) partners, all with different information needs (van Ladesteijn, 2000).

Assessing the Success of PAN Parks

PAN Parks started as a concept in 1997, and for the ensuing years has been in the development and piloting stage, mainly involving the organisation of internal structures, development of systems for compliance assessment, and establishment of links with potential candidates. It would appear that the experience to date of candidate parks has been positive for those in need of expertise in natural area and tourism management, which are mainly located in the more remote parts of Northern Europe, or in Eastern Europe. Those in wealthier areas, and with more experience in these areas, however, appear to be questioning the benefits of their involvement. Indeed, one potential fate of PAN Parks is for it to become a programme that engenders a more proactive approach to park management in the less developed parts of Europe.

Whether individual parks involved in the scheme become more sustainable than they otherwise would have been without input from PAN Parks is difficult to assess. It can be said, however, that principles 4 and 5 of the scheme that concern the engagement of local communities and organisations, along with businesses, in the development of national areas are in line with the more progressive attitudes evident amongst some park managers. They also reflect the perceptions on conservation embodied in Natura 2000. Only once PAN Parks has progressed to the point where it has certified a number of parks, can the question of how successful or otherwise it has been in enhancing standards of natural area conservation, while at the same time facilitating tourism development of such areas, be answered. This question would make the subject of a worthwhile future study.

3

Perspectives on Sustainable Tourism

Any discussion of sustainable tourism, or tourism that respects and preferably enhances the environmental and sociocultural carrying capacity of a destination, must take into account the physical and cultural characteristics of the destinations that are being considered. Insularity is one such characteristic that can significantly influence the attainment of sustainable tourism outcomes. This chapter specifically considers the status of sustainable tourism in the South Pacific region, a macro-region notable for its exaggerated insularity The first of four major sections outlines the physical and human geographical characteristics of the study region, and this is followed by a generalised discussion of the regional tourism sector. The third section uses level of intensity as a basis for examining a variety of South Pacific destination in order to assess the evidence for and against the existence of sustainable tourism practices. The fourth and final section considers the options for tourism in the study region in light of the preceding material. The chapter does not purport to be inclusive or all encompassing in terms of the South Pacific destinations which are described or discussed. Furthermore, it does not attempt to draw any definitive conclusions about the presence or absence of sustainable tourism, but rather is intended to raise important issues for further investigation.

The Geographical Context

Any meaningful discussion of tourism in the South Pacific must be preceded by a consideration of the region's broader geographic, historic, economic and sociocultural characteristics. These constitute an 'external environment' to tourism that effectively determines whether sustainable tourism can be achieved and even if so, whether such a mode of tourism has any relevance if this broader context does not adhere to the precepts of sustainability. In other words, the opportunities and constraints inherent in this external environment profoundly influence the likelihood of achieving a meaningful state of 'sustainable tourism,' even after recognising all the ambiguities and difficulties that are inherent in the latter term. Another propose of this review is to emphasise the status of the South Pacific as a highly complex region in which the sub-regions (and destination within those sub-regions) display considerable internal diversity.

Physically, the South Pacific study region can be divided into Polynesia and Micronesia on the one hand, and Melanesia on the other. The first two sub-regions are characterised by extreme insularity, consisting of small island entities separated by enormous expanses of ocean. In contrast, Melanesia comprises large islands clustered within relatively compressed archipelagos the account for 97.9 per cent (542,230 square kilometres) of all land in the study region (Table 1). Melanesia is also distinguished within the South Pacific for its variety of landforms, relatively undisturbed habitat, and high levels of biodiversity and endemism. The entire study region is susceptible to cyclones, while seismic and volcanic activity are characteristic of plate boundary areas such as Papua New Guinea, the Solomon Islands, Vanuatu and Tonga.

The differences between Melanesia and the other sub-regions extend to human geography. Only 16 per cent of the regional population is located within Polynesia (8639 square kilometres) and Micronesia (3097 square kilometre) (Table 1). However, the lack of

Table 1. Land area and population in the South Pacific.

By state and region	*Land area (Km²)*	*Population 1998 (000s)*	*Population Km²*
Papua New Guinea	461,690	4598.8	10.0
Fiji	18,270	802.6	43.9
Solomon Islands	28,450	441.0	15.5
New Caledonia (Fr)	19,060	194.2	10.2
Vanuatu	14,760	185.2	12.5
Melanesia (Total)	**542,230**	**6222.8**	**11.5**
Guam (US)	541	148.1	273.8
Fed. States Micronesia	702	129.7	184.8
Kiribati	717	84.0	117.2
Northern Marianas (US)	477	66.6	139.6
Marshall Is.	181	63.0	348.1
Palau	458	18.1	39.5
Nauru	21	10.5	500.0
Micronesia (Total)	**3097**	**520.0**	**167.9**
French Polynesia (Fr)	3941	237.8	60.3
Samoa	2860	224.7	78.6
Tonga	748	108.2	144.7
Wallis and Futuna Is. (Fr)	274	15.0	54.7
Niue (NZ)	260	1.6	6.2
Cook Islands (NZ)	240	20.0	83.3
American Samoa (US)	199	62.1	312.1
Pitcairn is. (UK)	47	<1.0	1.0
Norfolk I. (Aus)	34	2.2	64.7
Tuvalu	26	10.4	400.0
Tokelau (NZ)	10	1.4	140.0
Polynesia (Total)	**8639**	**683.4**	**79.1**
South Pacific (Total)	**553,966**	**7426.2**	**13.4**

land in these sub-regions results in population densities higher by an order of magnitude than those of Melanesia (Table 1), and a higher degree of human-induced environmental degradation both on land and sea. Ethnically, each of the sub-regions is associated with a separate indigenous racial group after which each region is named, allowing for a significant degree of intermixture and acculturation as a result of ongoing historical contact, particularly in transitional border islands. Pre-European elements of these cultures remain robust, given that the South Pacific was one of the last regions to be formally incorporated into the global capitalist economy. This is especially true with regard to language and communal land tenure systems, while other attributes, such as religion, and economics, have been profoundly changed during the past 150 years of intensive European contact and subsequent acculturation. Fiji and New Caledonia are the only two entities where non-indigenous groups are roughly comparable in population to indigenous people. As a region, the South Pacific is characterised by high fertility rates and, despite high rates of out-migration, steady population increase and resultant added pressure on natural resources. Politically, the South Pacific shares with the Caribbean the distinction of having the highest concentration of dependent political units (i.e., ten remaining dependencies), indicating that this region is also the last to be experiencing the formal de-colonisation process. Melanesia has no remaining dependencies, but is characterised by a high level of political instability, as evidenced by recent upheavals in the Solomon Islands and Fiji.

In the South Pacific elements of physical geography, human geography and history have conspired to produce fragile environments and weak economic structures that are not indicative of, or conducive to, sustainable economic development in the western sense. Bertram and Watters characterise the South Pacific as a region where the MIRAB syndrome (i.e. *migration, remittances, aid* and *bureaucracy*) is prevalent, reflecting a reliance upon a narrow range of economic activities, and subsequently severe trade deficits and dramatic fluctuation in economic performance. The MIRAB syndrome is most apparent on small outlying atolls, where insularity and isolation are exaggerated, but is also evident in Melanesia despite that sub-region's much greater endowment of natural resources. In terms of per capita GNP, many South Pacific states rank among the world's poorest, with Papua New-Guinea, the Solomon Islands, Vanuatu, Kiribati, Samoa, the Marshall Island and Micronesia all being below US$ 2600 following adjustments for purchasing power parity.

The Tourism Context

At a regional scale, the South Pacific is over-represented as an inbound tourist destination, with 0.13 per cent of the world's population, but 0.5 per cent of all international stayovers. This observation, however, is rendered all but meaningless by the highly skewed internal distribution of the sector, which is overwhelmingly dominated by inbound as opposed to domestic tourists. Just two small destinations, Guam and the Northern Marianas (the island of Saipan, specifically), account for almost 60 per cent of all stayovers, and this figure increases to over 80 per cent with the addition of Fiji and French Polynesia (Table 2). Tourist arrivals in the remaining eighteen destinations, and indeed in the numerous peripheral islands of the last three named destinations, indicate a more incipient level of tourism development, and a much higher level of return visits by former residents who tend to stay in local residences and spend less money. Interrelated factors that have contributed to this situation include isolations, the lack of infrastructure and accommodation, the scarcity of freehold land, and a lack of interest among potential investors, due in part to the presence of intervening opportunities in more accessible and established regional destinations such as Hawaii and Okinawa. In this context, Guam and Saipan can be seen as anomalies that have benefited from their proximity to Japan, the provision of infrastructure and other services as an outcome of World War II and their status as US dependencies.

Given the economic context, it is not surprising that South Pacific states and dependencies have been paying increased attention to tourism as a vehicle for helping to overcome the MIRAB syndrome and bringing into effect sustained economic development. This

Table 2. International stayover arrivals in the South Pacific.

By state and region	*1991 (000s)*	*1998 (000s) (A)*	*Percentage of region: 1998*	*Tourist resident ratio 1998(B)*	*Intensity category (AB)*	*Tourism as estimated percentage of GDP*
Fiji	259	371.4	13.7	0.46	HL	17
New Caledonia	81	103.8	3.8	0.53	LL	3
PNG	37	67.5	2.5	0.01	LL	< 1
Vanuatu	40	52.1	1.9	0.23	LL	15
Solomon Islands	11	13.2	0.5	0.03	LL	2
Melanesia (Total)	**428**	**608.0**	**22.4**	**0.10**		
Guam	737	1137.0	41.8	7.68	HH	na
Northem Marianas	422	490.2	18.0	7.36	HH	50
Palau	33	64.2	2.4	3.55	LH	10
Micronesia	8	11.0*	0.4	0.08	LL	na
Marshall Is.	7	6.4	0.2	0.10	LL	5
Kiribati	3	5.4	0.2	0.06	LL	1
Nauru	1	1.0	<0.1	0.10	LL	na
Micronesia (Total)	**1210**	**1715.2**	**63.1**	**3.30**		
French Polynesia	121	188.3	6.9	0.79	HH	23
Samoa	35	77.9	2.9	0.35	LL	13
Cook Islands	40	48.6	1.8	2.43	LH	23
Norfolk I.	na	29.0	1.1	13.18	LH	na
Tonga	22	27.1	1.0	0.25	LL	6
American Samoa	18	21.3†	0.8	0.34	LL	5
Niue	1	1.7	0.1	1.06	LH	18
Tuvalu	1	1.1	<0.1	0.11	LL	na
Pitcaim Is.	na	na	na	na	LL	na
Tokelau	na	na	na	na	LL	na
Wallis and Futuna Is.	na	na	na	na	LL	na
Polynesia (Total)	**238**	**395.0**	**14.5**	**0.58**		
South Pacific (Total)	**1876**	**2718.2**	**100.0**	**0.37**		

Sources : *Europe World Year Book*, 1997 (GDP states); *WTO*, 1997; 1998 data for Nauru from Fagence, 1999.

*1997 data.

†1997 data.

attention is not new. Tourism was already included as a component of development strategies in the late colonial and early post-independence period, when it was standard practice of uncritically endorse the sector as a panacea for underdeveloped countries in general. Jafari (1989), accordingly, refers to this as the era of the advocacy platform. By the 1970s, however, the negative impacts of poorly regulated tourism became more obvious, prompting widespread criticism of the sector and the emergence of cautionary platform. Along with the Caribbean, the South Pacific emerged as a focal point of this critique, with references to tourism as a 'new kind of sugar' and a 'pleasure plantation.' The well-known and often-tested destination life cycle model of Butler (1980), which foresees stagnation and decline as the likely outcomes of unregulated tourism development, may be seen as the culmination of the cautionary platform.

Actual attempts to put forward more benign models of tourism development are associated with the era of the adaptancy platform in the 1980s, which gave rise to supposedly more appropriate options such as 'alternative tourism,' 'ecotourism' and, of course, 'sustainable tourism.' Explicit within this platform was the view that mass tourism was inherently bad and smallscale alternative tourism (i.e., tourism that is deliberately structured to contrast with conventional mass tourism) inherently good for small underdeveloped Pacific and Caribbean islands in particular. Alternative, tourism and ecotourism, therefore, were equated with sustainable tourism. This perspective is now being challenged by the 'knowledge-based platform,' which espouses a less ideological and more scientific perspective toward tourism (though adoption of a scientific approach may itself be seen as an ideological decision). From this platform, mass tourism and alternative tourism can both be either sustainable or unsustainable, depending on the circumstances that pertain to any particular destination.

Sustainable Tourism in the South Pacific

Since early 1990s, virtually all South Pacific destinations have declared their interest in, and commitment to, sustainable tourism. Many planners and academics still adhere to the pro-alternative tourism biases of the adaptancy platform and argue that this is the only means for attaining sustainable tourism development in the region. Yet by disassociating scale from sustainability, the knowledge-based platform holds that the attainment of sustainability does not necessarily depend on adherence to alternative tourism. Moreover, it has been argued that conventional mass tourism, in theory, confers sustainability-related advantages of scale that are not possible in alternative tourism. Intensity is used in this section as a criterion for placing South Pacific countries and dependencies into categories for discussion purposes, but given the above debate, no assumptions are made as to the advantages of high or low intensity relative to the attainment of sustainable outcomes. Rather, the evidence from the destinations themselves will be used to make such assessments. For classification and discussion purposes, 'intensity' is construed as a variable that arises from different combinations of absolute and relative criteria. The total number of inbound stayover arrivals represents the former while the latter is represented by the stayover/resident ratio. Of course, these are not perfect criteria since, amongst other reasons, returning former residents (who comprises a high proportion of stayover arrivals in destinations such as Tonga and Niue) are likely to stay in 'local' areas and blend into the local community, thereby not contributing to an obvious intensification effect. Cruiseship excursionists are omitted since this subsector occupies a relatively minor role in the region. Rankings of the listed destinations for both variables revealed gaps in the data that provide a logical basis for separating 'high' from 'low' intensity destinations. In both cases, the gap occurred between French Polynesia (188,300 arrivals and a ratio of 0.79) and New Caledonia (103,800 and 0.53) (Table 2).

Classified accordingly, the destinations fall into four possible categories: low traffic/low ratio (LL), low traffic/high ratio (LH); high traffic/low ratio (HL), and high traffic/high ratio (HH) (Table 2). Although all destinations, and especially the archipelagic states, have significant internal variations in the intensity of tourism, there are several reasons for basing classification on the entire state or dependency. Firstly, it is usually difficult to obtain even basic tourism data (except perhaps for accommodation) at the sub-national level. Secondly, it is not clear at what sub-national scale the classification should be made if this approach is adopted, since individual peripheral islands of a state may themselves display significant internal variations. Thirdly, whatever the internal differences, all regions and people within a single state or dependency are commonly affected in some ways by the national tourism industry, through the right to move internally in order to obtain employment, and through the dissemination of benefits resulting from tourism revenues. Though rejected as a basis for classification, internal variations nevertheless will still be recognised and taken into account, particularly in the section where options are discussed.

Low Traffic/Low Ratio (LL) Destinations

Low intensity destinations account for a clear majority to South Pacific states and dependencies, with several, such as the Pitcairn Islands and Tokel'au, having virtually no tourist arrivals or facilities at all (Tokelau Apia Liaison Office, Samoa, personal communication, 1997). For those with at least some level of tourism development, the evidence does not always point toward sustainable practice or outcomes. The colonial heritage of most islands and the concomitant positioning of 'local' expatriates in positions of influence, for example, resulted in the marginalisation of indigenous people during the 'involvement' phase of the tourism cycle throughout Melanesia. This trend was, and still is, exacerbated by the lack of skilled locals in countries such as Tuvalu or Palau that have fewer people than a small English country town. A very similar situation pertained to other colonised small islands outside of the Pacific, such as the Caribbean island of Antigua. The situation has improved somewhat in the post-independence era, though businesses owned by ni-Vanuatu (native people of Vanuatu) still accounted for less than 10 per cent of total expenditure within Vanuatu's accommodation sector during the mid-1990s.

The alleged dispersal of the tourism sector during the early stages of the cycle is often deemed to be congruent with sustainable tourism in that the resultant benefits are more accessible to a wider sector of the local population. Moreover, carrying capacities are not unduly stressed by over-concentrations of activity within specific tourism districts. Again, the evidence from the LL destinations is contrary, as urban areas are substantially over-represented as locations for tourist accommodation. On Pohnpei (a Federated State of Micronesia), virtually all hotels are located in the capital city of Kolonia, while almost two-thirds of registered accommodation in Papua New Guinea is found in the three largest urban centres. This pattern owes to a combination of factors, including the prevalence of business-related tourism, the concentration of functions and services in urban areas, and the status of capital cities as international and internal gateways. Such concentrations, however, cannot automatically be considered unsustainable. Unlike beach environments, urban areas already accommodate a broad array of high-density activity within a highly modified and relatively cosmopolitan environment that usually has the infrastructure capacity to cope with this level of activity.

The Butler-type resort cycle implies that negative sociocultural outcomes are liable to occur as a function of increased tourism development. However, problems such as a pronounced demonstration effect, the commoditisation of local culture and the entrenchment of the power and wealth of the local 'Big Men' are already apparent in incipient destinations such as the Solomon Islands. The burning of the Anuha Resort in 1998 by customary Solomon Islands landowners, though cited as an isolated event, is indicative of the resident antagonism that might be expected to result in the later, not earlier, stages of tourism development. Similar negative sociocultural developments occurred in Tonga as early as the 1970s, while inter-clan rivalries in the Tufi region of Papua New Guinea occurred because of tourism in the early 'involvement' stages of tourism development. These examples are not meant to suggest that attitudes toward tourism in all LL destinations are antagonistic or that all of the affected cultures and societies are being undermined. Rather, they indicate that such destinations are not immune to negative outcomes just because tourism is relatively undeveloped and smallscale, or 'alternative.' The sustainability of tourism at this incipient stage can also be negatively affected by external factors such as logging, which in the Solomon Islands is estimated to be undertaken at a level three times in excess of a sustainable harvest. In Nauru, environmental problems focus around the mining-related devastation that has affected almost the entire interior of the island. An additional dissuasive factor for tourism development in the Solomon Islands was the outbreak of civil war in 2000 and the concomitant descent into political and social anarchy. Whether environmental or sociopolitical, such hostile external environments could ensure that the destination does not progress beyond tourism incipience within the foreseeable future.

Substantial fluctuations in the level of tourist arrivals are often seen as conflicting with sustainability, yet characterise many LL destinations simply because a small drop in arrivals can translate into a large relative decrease when the overall visitor base numbers are low. In Tonga, the lowest visitation month in just 45 per cent of the peak month of December (3579). For Vanuatu, the same calculation revealed a figure of 54 per cent for 1996 (2639 in February, 4813 in September). Such variations are partly climate-related, but also reflect the large impacts exercised by specific events, such as a monopolistic airline's decision to reduce flight frequency, on small volumes of traffic. As a result, LL destinations tend to experience high levels of vulnerability and uncertainty in their visitor flows, for reasons other than seasonality. Exacerbating this vulnerability is a common dependency on a small number of tourist markets. For example, the two principal markets in Tonga accounted for 53 per cent of all stayover arrivals in 1995, while the equivalent statistic for Vanuatu was 70 per cent in 1996 (with Australia alone contributing 58 %).

Low Traffic/High Ratio (LH) Destination

Low traffic/high ratio destinations receive small absolute numbers of tourists in relation to the threshold established above, but still produce relatively large tourist/resident ratios because of the small local population. The Cook Islands, Niue, Norfolk Island and Palau are the four South Pacific destinations that fall into this category. In all four cases, the tourist/resident ratio exceeds 1.0, and at least 10 per cent of GDP is represented by tourism. The Cook Islands is one of the most tourism-dependent LH destinations and resembles a more intensively developed destination as well from the perspective of foreign participation. External interests control just over half (50.6%) of accommodation rooms, with the proportion increasing to 58 per cent on the main island of Rarotonga. One surprising development, however, is the decline of market concentration as the destinations has become more developed. Contrary to the expectations of the destination life cycle, the dependency of the Cook Islands on its primary market (New Zealand) has actually declined from 55.7 to 21.8 per cent between 1979 and 1995, largely as a result of growth in Asian origin regions. The tourism sector of Niue, in contrast, is marked by extremes in market dependency and fluctuation. In 1995, New Zealand supplied 83.5 per cent of all arrivals. The number of visitors during the lowest month of that year represented only 20 per cent of the traffic arriving in the busiest month (80 versus 410 visitors).

High Traffic/Low Ratio (HL) Destination

Fiji is the only South Pacific destination where a large absolute number of stayover arrivals is offset by a low tourist/resident ratio, owing to the country's relatively large resident population. Such generalisations, however, mask the actual complexity of the Fijian tourism sector, which ranges from mass resort tourism along some coastal areas of Viti Levu to exclusive resort island tourism, urban tourism (in Suva) and village based ecotourism. Segmented in this way, all categories are represented in Fiji, and it is fair to characterise this destination as a microcosm of South Pacific tourism in general. Like the Cook Islands, inbound markets are becoming more rather than less diverse, with the two primary markets accounting for 57.2 per cent and 41.8 per cent of all stayovers in 1980 and 1993, respectively. Another departure from the usual social impact assumptions is the finding by King *et al.* that Fijians in the vicinity of Nadi, with its concentration of beach-based resorts, tended to express favourable attitudes about the tourism industry.

The small, exclusive resorts, usually located on small offshore islands, are also complex with respect to their relationship with sustainability. The Turtle Island Resort offers a case in point. On the one hand, this resort caters to a very wealthy elite (= a very strong wealth differential between host and guest), is owned by an expatriate American millionaire, and requires its employees to remain isolated from their families for extended periods of time. However, the Resort has also engaged in a major programme of vegetation rehabilitation on the island, provides almost 100 jobs, and has a strategy to encourage Fijian participation at the managerial level. It also uses solar power to provide much of its energy requirements, and has established an eye clinic and other medical services for the residents of the adjacent islands. At least in this case, the positive effects would seem to outweigh the negative impacts, although no generalisations about exclusive isolated resorts should follow. A more serious issue for Fijian tourism as a whole is chronic political instability, the latest crisis being the 2,000 coup attempt by George Speight that resulted in a dramatic decline in visitor arrivals. Notably, Turtle Island was specifically targeted for takeover by indigenous Fijian coup supporters over issues of land rights, though the extent to which associated activism was legitimate or politically opportunistic is unclear.

High Traffic/High Ratio (HH) Destination

Only two South Pacific destinations, Guam and the Northern Marianas, have large absolute number of tourist visitors and high tourist/resident ratios arising from low resident populations. In several superficial respects, both destinations conform to the more mature phases of the resort cycle. Market concentration in Guam, for example, is indicated by Japan's 75 per cent share of stayovers, which increases to 89 per cent with the addition of Korea. The comparable statistic for the Northern Marianas is 85 per cent (62% from Japan and 23% from Korea). Foreign participation in the tourism sector, another indication of maturity according to Butler is also very high in both destinations, with 15 of 30 hotels (with 50 % of all rooms) in Guam having Japanese general managers. The same situation pertains to seven of the ten largest hotels in the Northern Marianas.

Structurally, hotel size and room inventories are the largest within the study region. The average hotel size in Guam is 253 rooms, and the island provided 7,601 rooms in 1997. The Northern Marianas contained 3,847 hotel rooms in 1997, virtually all located on Saipan. While these figures already raise concerns because of the small physical size of each destination, further increases are likely. As of 1995, the number of hotel rooms approved by government of Guam was equivalent to the total amount in existence or under construction at that time. If announced or potential rooms are added, the inventory could increase to over 26,000 rooms (Table 3). Among the approved hotels are two that each provides over 1,000 rooms (Marbo Cave Resort, at 1,200, and Nansay Resort, at 1,100). The hotel sector in Guam, as in most intensive beach resorts, is highly concentrated, with 83 per cent of all rooms (and about one-half of all approved hotels) located along a short stretch of coastline at Tumon village. However, an equally vigorous process of golf course expansion (Table 3) enhances the influence of tourism as a consumer of land. On Saipan, 69 per cent of all hotel rooms are located on a five-mile expanse of beach in the southwest of the island. While no statistics are available indicating the contribution of tourism to Guam's GDP, this can be inferred from employment data. Of 48,980 jobs in total as of March 1997, 11,892 (24%) were directly related to tourism, and another 8,766 (18%) were indirectly related to tourism, for 20,657 in total (42%). The resultant figure is not inconsistent with the GDP statistic for tourism in the Northern Marianas.

Clearly, the current and potential intensity levels of tourism in the two HH destinations are impressive and of obvious concern to those wishing to develop a sustainable tourism industry, especially when other factors such as ownership and market concentration are taken into account. However, just as some of the characteristics of LL destinations do not appear coherent with sustainability, certain traits of the HH destinations appeal compatible. With respect to seasonality, the lowest visitation month in Guam, calculated as a mean value from 1992 to 1996, is 78 per cent of the peak visitation month (April = 79,800; March = 1,01,900). The low/high month ratio for Saipan is a similar 84 per cent. Resident reactions to tourism on Guam, as well, do not indicate antagonism. Although solicited from only one segment of the market, an exit survey of US visitors in December 1996 revealed 'friendliness and courteousness of the people of Guam' as the local attribute given the highest rating on a Likert-type scale (6.1 of 7.0). As for the physical carrying capacity of the island, high concentrations of tourism facilities and large hotel complexes may compensate in some degree for their obvious local stresses (high traffic, 'heat island' effect, induced housing development for hotel workers, etc.) in several ways. These include the provision of 'economies of scale' that allow for the effective management of waste, and the minimisation of space required to house the tourist population (*i.e.*, upward instead of outward, and in one small area instead of distributed throughout the island). A strong tourism industry may also in theory possess lobbying capabilities that prevent competing resource stakeholders (*e.g.*, fishing and agriculture) from undertaking activities that undermine the attractiveness of tourism resources.

Tourism Options

The South Pacific tourism industry can be summarised as highly skewed, with most destinations being characterised by low visitor numbers and low tourist/resident ratios. Only two destinations exhibit the opposite tendency. Intensity, however, is clearly no a priori indicator of sustainability. Low visitation levels are inherently vulnerable to extreme fluctuation, and tourism, even in its incipient stages is inevitably influenced in a negative way by the MIRAB syndrome and by longstanding patterns of dependency with 'mother' countries. Islands with low levels of tourism development, moreover, tend to possess rudimentary infrastructure that equates with low carrying capacity and subsequent threats to environmental sustainability despite small visitor intakes. That low intensity tourism does not automatically equate with sustainable tourism, therefore, should come as no surprise. The question of sustainability will always be mediated by the realities of the small island syndrome of underdevelopment and by a longstanding regional degradation.

Sustainable Mass Tourism

If this impeding impact of the small island syndromes is granted, then the pursuit of higher intensity tourism may be a rational option for some South Pacific destinations or portions thereof, since there is often no 'unspoiled paradise' to be undermined by the development of mass tourism. To the contrary, it is the more tourism-intensive destinations that display higher prosperity levels on the basis of per capita GDP (allowing for anomalies such as the phosphate producing country of Nauru). This endorsement, however, is not unconditional, and supposes that intensive tourism is not appropriate in all location and that its implementation be carefully regulated so as to minimise any further disruption to the destination's economy, culture or physical environment. Preferably, the onus should also be placed on the various stakeholders, and on large corporations in particular, to contribute to the gradual amelioration of these disrupted sectors and spaces. Such could be a pre-condition for anyone, local or expatriate, for obtaining permission to establish tourism-related facilities.

Deliberate 'Alternative Tourism' (DAT)

Although tourism scenarios are continuous in nature with respect to their intensity, it is still useful for conceptual purposes to contrast 'mass tourism' with 'alternative tourism' as ideal types situated at either end of the tourism spectrum. Alternative tourism, as described above, was conceived in the early 1980s as a mode of tourism deliberately structured to contrast with the supposedly unsustainable characteristics of conventional mass tourism. Accordingly, it was ideally characterised among other things by smallscale, local control, architecture that is congruent with the local culture and physical environment, and interactions with locals that are equitable and mutually supportive. A particular destination scenario can be said to gravitate, to a greater or lesser extent, toward one ideal type (*i.e.*, alternative tourism) or the other (*i.e.* unsustainable mass tourism). At the less intensive end of the spectrum, most South Pacific destinations resemble 'alternative tourism' in at least some respects, though patterns of ownership, imports, market concentration and seasonality more typical of intensive destinations have already been identified. Clearly, the resemblance to alternative tourism in most of these destinations is superficial, as there is seldom any regulatory environment in place to ensure, as far as possible, that principle of local participation, environmental sustainability, etc., are followed. These places, essentially, are merely in the early stages of the (modified small island) destination life cycle, and accordingly can be described as circumstantial alternative tourism (CAT) destinations. This would seem to apply, for example, to Papua New Guinea, where 85 per cent of the 14,000 short-term visitor arrivals in 1995 had visited nature based attractions, but where little exists in the way of a formal ecotourism structure that adheres to core criteria of nature-focused attractions, learning outcomes, and sustainability.

Several scenarios are possible for CAT destinations. In most instances, they will remain as such because there is no demand for any further tourism-related development is impractical due to inaccessibility or other factors. A second possibility sees these destinations following the S-curve trajectory that characterises the Butler-type destination life cycle. A third scenario is the 'instant resort' phenomenon, wherein the area is earmarked for planned large-scale resort development (*e.g.*, Cancun in Mexico). In both cases, a very rapid transitions from LL status to LH or HH status is possible because of the small resident population. A fourth scenario entails the establishment of a regulatory environment that steers the destination toward the principles of alternative (and hence small-scale sustainable) tourism. Places that adopt this approach can be described as 'deliberate alternative tourism' (DAT) destinations. Such a strategy is implicit in the planning of many South Pacific destinations. Applied at the sub-national level, such as in mountainous interiors or peripheral islands, it may be designated as a regional DAT strategy (or R–DAT). Applied to an entire country or dependency, the term comprehensive DAT (C-DAT) may employed, as discussed in the following sub-section.

Comprehensive DAT (C-DAT) Destinations

C-DAT destinations are rare, although Dominica and Bhutan would probably qualify if a global survey were to be conducted. In the study region, emergent C-DAT destinations include the Federated Micronesian State of Pohnpei, whose apparent pursuit of an environmentally sound, ecotourism-style policy (Office of Tourism & Parks, Pohnpei, personal communication, 1997), it should be noted, is motivated by the lack of beaches capable of supporting mass tourism. Nevertheless, pressure to pursue mass tourism is arising from concerns over the impending termination of special post-independence financial aid from the US government, and from calculations revealing that an annual visitor intake of 50,000 is necessary to compensate for the loss of those funding revenues.

The Niue Strategic Development Plan identifies tourism as the sector with the greatest potential to facilitate sustainable development. A village-based strategy is being proposed as the centrepiece of a policy to 'develop a sustainable tourism sector whose activities are compatible with Niue's unique environment and culture, which are the country's principal tourism attractions.' Tourism on Niue thus far is not seen as involving any substantial negative environmental or sociocultural impacts. Samoa is somewhat more evolved in the C-DAT direction, having already established such relevant mechanisms as the National Ecotourism Programme and the Samoan Ecotourism Network.

Regional DAT (R-DAT) Destinations

Several larger South Pacific destinations are initiating strategies that explicitly recognise a role for both mass tourism and deliberate alternative tourism. For example, Vanuatu's Tourist Development Master Plan emphasises a hierarchical spatial structure of 'Primary' tourist destinations (international/regional gateway and port, larger volume of visitation) and 'Longer Term' tourist destinations. The latter are characterised by local or regional airports, limited infrastructure, small-scale tourist facilities, retained local customs and village lifestyles, and controlled visitation to environmentally and culturally sensitive areas. The latter tend to involve the smaller peripheral islands.

In Fiji, the R-DAT concept has long been implicit in an 'islands policy' that discourages large-scale tourism in peripheral island locations, a concept that has also been practised in the Bahamas with respect to the 'Family Islands' relative to Grand Bahama and Nassau, and in Trinidad relative to Tobago. While 'tourism resort islands' (such as Turtle Island Resort) are one option, most of these areas are designated as local subsistence islands where only smallscale development will be permitted. In contrast, largescale tourism is being fostered in certain districts of the main island, including the Coral Coast and Nadi. Other districts of this island, particularly in the interior, are focusing upon alternative tourism and smallscale ecotourism in particular. One example among several is occurring at Abaca village in the Koronayitu forest of western Viti Levu. Its establishment in the early 1990s coincided with the formation of a national park in the area. Abaca village initially constructed a traditional lodge to accommodate twelve visitors, and in 1993, the Abaca Ecotourism Co-operative Society Limited was registered to formalise the participation and ownership structure of the venture. Subsequently, another village was added to the scheme, and others have expressed an interest in joining. Each participating village is expected to dedicate a portion of their communal land to the national park, and is then entitled to hold shares in a company which promotes ecotourism in the area. In addition to the ecotourism revenues, tangible benefits to Abaca so far have included the formation of a medicinal plant arboretum, a tree seedling nursery, and the use of the tourism vehicle to transport children to school.

Part of the success of the Abaca venture is attributed to the village's proximity to the concentration of tourism activity at Nadi, and its subsequent linkages with the mass tourism sector of that area. Accordingly, the cultivation of such opportunities as an 'add-on' to the mainstay resort product has long been a feature of the Fijian tourism sector. More recently, such relationships in Fiji and elsewhere are being formally recognised and promoted as a matter of mutual advantage to both types of tourism. Thus, the ideal outcome of the R-DAT strategy is the creation of synergies and symbioses between alternative and mass tourism, a possibility that is supported by Ayala and Weaver amongst others.

Conclusion

Evidence from the diverse array of South Pacific tourist destinations suggests little or no correlation between scale of intensity and the presence of 'sustainable tourism.' Rather, the apparent presence or absence of sustainability, or indications of same, is dependent upon the unique circumstances that pertain to any given destination and the management responses that are made to these circumstances. Accordingly, there is no basis for supposing that tourism in intensively developed Saipan or Guam is any less sustainable than the incipient sector that characterises Tuvalu or the Wallis and Futuna Islands, where government, infrastructure and society in general are ill-equipped to cope with even a small increase in arrivals. Complicating the issue of sustainability is the possibility that a destination may indicate this trait in some characteristics (*e.g.*, is environmentally sound) but not others (*e.g.*, is not locally controlled), thereby raising the question as to whether the destination is 'sustainable' in an overall sense. Moreover, a characteristic that appears unsustainable in itself may have sustainable consequences. For example, the transformation of land on Guam to golf courses is associated with environmental problems and the loss of agricultural self-sufficiency. However, these golf courses may generate enough revenue to allow the importation of diverse foodstuffs and to facilitate remedial environmental measures. Increased importation of food, in turn, might increase dependency, though the alternative to dependency may be abject poverty. Similarly, the concentration of tourism within a small area of Saipan (a characteristic of destination life cycle maturity that is usually regarded as negative) reduces the need for sprawling tourism facilities in other parts of the island. Concurrently, it offers conditions conducive to cost-effective and environmentally beneficial site hardening, such as the installation of tertiary sewage treatment that depends upon high volumes of waste production.

An equally important issue is whether the concept of sustainability, and concomitant planning option as described above, can be seriously considered from a single-sector perspective. Various external environments over which tourism exercises little or no influence profoundly affect this sector in a direct or indirect way. The MIRAB syndrome is especially relevant to the South Pacific as is, unfortunately, the apparent increase in political instability and environmental degradation. Thus, for example, while deliberate alternative tourism appears to be emerging in the Solomon Islands, any judgements about its sustainability and longevity are rendered effectively meaningless by the fact that civil war and rapacious logging practices make most human activity in the Solomon Islands as a whole unsustainable. Adding to this uncertain environment, and especially relevant to South Pacific coastal areas and atoll-dominated countries such as Tuvalu and Kiribati, are the looming threats of rising sea levels and more numerous cyclones due to global warming. Whether sustainable mass tourism or deliberate alternative tourism is advocated for a particular South Pacific destination, the isolationist approach that typifies much planning and academic writing in the sector should therefore be rejected. The existing or potential impacts of these external environments must be taken into account when considering and implementing the options described above. Indeed, it can be argued that external environments are an omnipresent shadow theme that cannot be divorced from any considerations pertaining to sustainable tourism. In such a context, it is unlikely that any mode of tourism development, no matter how sustainable in itself, will serve on its own as a panacea for the persistent problems of South Pacific destinations.

4

How Sustainable is Mekong Tourism?

The Mekong River basin area with its peculiar history and great political, economic and social differences (the Mekong sub-region comprises Burma, Cambodia, Laos, Thailand, Vietnam and Yunnan in Southern China) is a region in which many of the issues and problems associated with tourism development can be observed. Until the 1980s, Thailand was the only country among the Mekong riparian states, which was fully integrated into the global capitalist system and had systematically developed a tourist industry to boost foreign exchange earnings and investment, as well as prestige in exchange for readily available cultural and natural resources. Over the last 20 years, tourist arrivals in Thailand have risen from one million to almost ten million annually.

Other Mekong countries remained more or less isolated from the rest of Southeast Asia after the Second World War because of post-colonial turmoil, the emergence of different political systems and American anti-communist warfare in Indochina. While Burma followed its own self-styled 'Burmese Path to Socialism,' China—and later Laos, Cambodia and Vietnam—were part of the socialist block. Travel to, from and within these countries was restricted, and much of the poor tourism–related infrastructure dated back to colonial times.

With the collapse of the state socialist block in the late 1980s, all Mekong nations decided to reform their economies and boost tourist as an industry in hope of quickly catching up with the Asian 'newly industrialised countries' (NICs). The growth of political and economic regionalism since the beginning of the 1990s has been vital for the emergence of several cooperation frameworks involving the Mekong Basin area, all of which prioritise the development of tourism and related infrastructure. Clearly, the recent tourism expansion into the Mekong sub-region has not happened incidentally or inevitably, but is the result of political will and substantial promotional efforts.

However, there is a clear tension in the Mekong Basin area between the requirement to meet the vast majority of the population who are poor and the prevailing policies of growth-driven economic development in the region. A central question is whether benefits from tourism can actually 'tickle down' and contribute to improve the living standard of disadvantaged social groups and indigenous peoples. Deprivation, uneven distribution of wealth, social inequalities and rapid depletion of natural resources, which set the stage for political, social, ethnic and ecological conflict, feature prominently in Mekong countries and make tourism a highly insecure industry.

Thailand has often been described as a negative tourism model because reckless development has resulted in the environmental degradation of many places, exacerbated economic inequalities and contributions to undesirable changes in society, such as the proliferation of the sex industry, AIDS, drug abuse, gambling, crime and cultural erosion. Government official and industry leaders framing the Mekong tourism development have acknowledged that the industry causes a plethora of problems and responded by incorporating the notions of 'sustainable tourism' into their policies and plans. They maintain that with improved planning and management, past mistakes can be avoided in new destinations.

Has a new era in tourism development begun that can reverse the negative trends so that Mekong's neighbouring countries will be spared from a tourism onslaught as experienced in Thailand? To answer this question, this chapter begins by examining regional tourism plans with a focus on the Greater Mekong Subregion (GMS) scheme initiated by the Asian Development Bank (ADB). The next section presents case studies that suggest that destructive tourism projects persist and are spreading throughout the Mekong basin area despite the constant rhetoric of sustainable tourism or ecotourism. Finally, the last section discusses the question of sustainability by taking into account some broader issues such as the impact of globalisation and lessons learned from the Asian economic crisis. It will be argued that the often ill-defined and reductionist sustainable tourism policies need to be replaced by holistic and people-centred development initiatives, if the goal is to work towards a sustainable future.

Tourism and Regional Development

Over the last decade all Mekong countries, except China, have become members of the Association of Southeast Asian Nations (ASEAN). This grouping has forged transborder economic cooperation programmes in the form of so-called 'growth triangles' with tourism development playing a prominent role. ASEAN even has its own Travel Association (ASEANTA) and declared 2002 as 'Visit ASEAN Year' under the theme 'ASEAN-Asia's Perfect 10 Paradise.' In 1996, ASEAN also set up its own working group on Mekong Basin Development Cooperation, with the major proposal under this initiative being the creation of a regional rail network for freight and passenger traffic, linking Singapore with Yunnan via Kuala Lumpur, Bangkok, Phnom Penh, Ho Chi Minh City and Hanoi.

The Mekong River Commission (MRC), under the auspices of the United Nations Development Programme (UNDP), has presented plans for the Mekong subregion, providing for 'economic growth together with environmental protection and cultural enrichment,' which includes tourism and related infrastructure development.

Another initiative is the Quadrangle for Economic Cooperation (QEC) which emphasises the improvement of land, water and air transport to promote tourism and trade. Formed in 1993 by a group of Thai business people and backed by influential Thai and Chinese politicians, the investors promoting the QEC have been especially eager to win concessions and attract funds to build roads and to develop tourism projects in the border areas of Thailand, Laos, Burma and Yunnan. Their plans involve the establishment of hotels, resorts, casinos and shopping centres, as well as 'model cultural villages' catering to adventurous 'ecotourists.'

However, the most prominent framework and prime mover of Mekong tourism is the ADB's GMS scheme.

The GMS Tourism Programme

Since its formation in 1992, the GMS initiative has endorsed more than 100 development projects in the field of transport, energy, tourism, telecommunication, environment and human resource development. While seven priority projects are directly related to tourism, 34 projects pertain to road, railway, water and air transport, and more than 50 deal with hydro-electricity generation. The GMS tourism working group has successfully garnered support from governments, international development agencies, large industry associations, as well as corporations to promote the subregion as a single tourism market.

Apart from the ADB, representatives of the six Mekong countries national tourism organisations (NTOs), international tourism association such as the World Tourism Organisation (WTO), the Pacific Asia Travel Association (PATA), ASEANTA, the UN Economic and Social Commission for Asia and the Pacific (ESCAP) and specialised UN agencies, have been involved in the GMS scheme. The Tourism Authority of Thailand (TAT), which has eagerly marketed Thailand as a 'gateway' to other Mekong countries, has also played a key role in the programme. Since 1996, TAT's office in Bangkok has accommodated the GMS tourism working group's secretariat known as the Agency for Coordinating Mekong Tourism Activities (AMTA).

Thailand also hosted the first Mekong Tourism Forum (MTF)—an annual event initiated by the GMS tourism working group—on the occasion of PATA's annual conference in Pttaya in April 1996. The MTF seeks possibilities to realise the 'Mekong Dream'—a concept designed by PATA to promote 'hassle-free' air and overland travel between Mekong countries since lack of accessibility, insufficient provisions for safety and difficult immigration regulations are seen by the industry as the main obstacles to regional tourism growth. In addition, to raise market awareness of the subregion's tourism resources, a worldwide campaign was launched at the MTF 1996 event to promote 30 cultural and natural tourist sites as 'Jewels of the Mekong.'

While working towards the removal of all barriers to travel in the Mekong Basin area (including physical, economic, organisational and legal barriers) that have so far discouraged foreign visitors and investors, the GMS initiative has emphasised 'sustainable development' and 'ecotourism' as worthy goals.

The Concept Plan for tourism development in the Greater Mekong Subregion 1999-2018, outlines the GMS strategy for the next 20 years. The major goal is to consolidate a "Mekong" cultural tourism, ecotourism and adventure tourism network by linking destinations, circuits and routes by the end of 2006. By 2018, it anticipates the GMS region will be 'one of the work's most important ecotourism and cultural tourism destinations' and a 'safe, accessible and "good value" (value of money) destination to experience the rich, natural, historical and cultural heritage of the peoples and places along and adjacent to the Mekong/Lancang River.'

Whereas ecotourism has nurtured notions of smallscale and controlled development, this plan aims at luring millions of additional international visitors to the Mekong subregion. Moreover, the list of priority projects proposed in the study are in line with the ADB's GMS mega-infrastructure programme and reflect a heavy emphasis on improving transportation systems involving navigation, highway construction and air route expansion.

The study says 'In the long-term, there will be emphasis on the creation of networks and gateways, transportation nodes and international standard facilities to accommodate all segments of the tourism market throughout the subregion.' In other words, there will be a focus on ecotourism and other alternative tourism forms such as 'village tourism' as long as there are major bottlenecks in infrastructure, which restrict large-scale tourism. Once all gates have been thrown open and the necessary facilities are in place, the plan is to tout for all shades of tourism, which ultimately means a shift to the development of mainstream mass tourism.

Meanwhile, it is widely acknowledged that the majority of the Bank's projects not only fail to meet their standards but are responsible for severe impacts on local communities and the environment.

For instance, the ADB put forward a proposal in 1996 for conservation management in watershed areas, which involves the gradual relocation of some 60 million mountain people in the sub-region. This massive resettlement programme has been legitimated with the claim that the widespread practice of shifting cultivation is a major cause for environmental destruction. In addition, a countless number of people are likely to be displaced and lose their traditional livelihoods by the Bank's more than 50 large dam projects.

According to ADB's belief, in the name of 'development' and 'poverty reduction,' local communities should abandon their traditional self-reliant and lifestyles and economic activities and turn to ecotourism as an alternative source of income in new locations. At the 9th Ministerial Meeting of the GMS Economic Cooperation Programme held in Manila in January 2000, Warren Evans, manager of the ADB's Environment Division, said 'We need to persuade hill communities that it's in their best interest to conserve rather than exploit natural resources by encouraging community participation in ventures such as ecotourism. They can discourage poachers and illegal loggers and operate sound tourist facilities.'

To introduce a comprehensive conservation programme that involves unprecedented mass evictions and inevitably degrades indigenous societies and cultures and then to offer tourism, as compensation is certainly one of the deepest ironies manifest in the GMS scheme. Much more so as tourism studies reveal that only a tiny proportion of tourism income actually reaches villagers. For instance, Minima Norbu Sherpa, a Nepalese representing the Worldwide Fund for Nature (WWF) argued at the ADB's first 'pro-poor tourism' seminar that in many cases, tourism's benefits do not make it to a country's outer reaches, even though those areas bear the impact of tourism. He cited Nepal's famous trekking areas as an example, where local people receive only 2 per cent of the tourism revenue.

Shiva Kumar, a development consultant based in Cambodia, concludes that the ADB and other donor agencies are primarily committed to creating a conducive environment for private corporations, rather than making a serious effort to lift weak and peripheral social groups out of poverty. 'In general, most projects developed by the donors, particularly the ADB and Japan, are capital-intensive while, at least in the short-term, labour-intensive projects are needed in these nations to challenge poverty. They have not been able to propose a plan to combine simultaneously, in a balanced and mutually reinforcing manner, economic growth with welfare, empowerment, cultural renaissance, social transformation and sustainability. These observations lead one to conclude that reduction of poverty is not the priority of these projects . . . . '

The following examples will demonstrate how damaging tourism activities have proliferated throughout the Mekong subregion over the past decade and posed severe pressure on local people and the environment.

Real-life Tourism Tales

(1) Mass 'ecotourism'—Thai Style

The rapid growth of tourism in Thailand during the 1970s and 1980s, particularly the upsurge of sex tourism, attracted severe criticism for its negative effects on Thai society.

> The impact of mass tourism in Thailand on the local people, their culture, natural resources and built environment has been substantial. Two striking effects of over-zealous profit-oriented tourism development efforts have been: (1) the disproportionate shift of

> capital to mass tourism-related construction and real estate developments at the expense of other sectors such as agriculture and small industry which are locally oriented; and (2) the promotion of over-consumption and excessive local resources with attendant new social and environmental pressures on local people and environments.

Coinciding with government and industry efforts to diversify Thailand's tourism products and to shed its worsening image as a 'spoilt' destination, has been the growing interest in 'ecotourism.' Acknowledging that tourism in the past had caused severe damage, Séree Wangpaichitr, the former TAT Governor, said in an interview with the *Bangkok Post* in June 1998: 'Ecotourism is the heart of long-term tourism development. He further argued that the mass tourism promotion by the TAT is not incompatible with ecotourism: The strategy is to 'distribute the mass of tourism to a great number of places so that resources will not be over-exploited while distributing the economic benefits to the wider public.'

Unfortunately, Thailand has longstanding experience with the mismanagement of forests, beaches, marine areas and other natural assets, and many hotels, resorts and other facilities have encroached on officially 'protected areas.' Repeated attempts by the Tourism Authority of Thailand (TAT) and the Royal Forestry Department (RFD) to open up national parks to private tourism businesses have elicited great controversy. Since 1997, the RFD has worded on a proposal to grant leases to operators of illegal tourist facilities on resort islands—a highly disputed plan that is expected to be approved by the government in the near future.

Many observers were amazed by the strong opposition of local residents and environmentalists towards the filming in 1999 of 20th Century Fox's movie 'The Beach,' starring Leonardo DiCaprio, in Phi Phi Island's National Park in Southern Thailand, which involved profound landscape changes at Maya Bay. But the protest actions and the related lawsuit filed by local government agencies and citizens against the film company and authorities, who gave permission to 're-design' a part of the park, need to be seen in the context of the fierce struggle for the protection and enforcement for Thailand's national park laws. Opponents repeatedly pointed out that 'The Beach' affair, which even led to an international boycott campaign against the Hollywood movie, was a precedence case, and the fight to save Maya Bay was not about just one island but about the fate of all parks in the country. The reason given by Thai officials for allowing the controversial film project to go ahead was to boost the country's tourism industry and income for local communities. But critics have warned that such incidents make a mockery of conservation efforts and the legal system, and set a bad example whereby commercialism can override any other issue in Thailand.

Indeed, the situation is worsening. Under the pretext of ecotourism promotion, the RFD has recently implemented massive tourism-related infrastructure projects—some involving logging operations—in parks countrywide, funded with loans from the World Bank and Japan. The frenzied construction of roads, parking lots, visitor centres, bungalows, camp sites and nature trails neatly coincided with the RFD's 'Visit National Park Year 2000' aimed at attracting more than 20 million domestic and international tourists to the parks during that year.

In Thailand, ecotourism development in nature reserves generally proceeds without the involvement of surrounding local communities in decision-making and without adequate discussion on who owns the land and natural resources, how land should be used, where and how tourist facilities should be built, visitor volume or regulation on tourist conduct; all of which has created and aggravated ecological problems and conflict between the government, private industry and communities. For instance, when the RFD proposed to increase the land area protected by national parks in northern Thailand a few years ago, some 10,000 people—primarily from ethnic minority groups—rejected the RFD's plans to evict than from their lands and held street demonstrations in the city of Chiang Mai.

The social injustice inherent in 'tourism-cum-conservation' projects is evident as they stop the access to land and natural resources of one social group—poor villagers who have often inhabited the area for generations—and open these areas for other groups—investors and paying ecotourists.

Whenever the Thai economy is in trouble, the government resorts to tourism as its saviour, with agriculture and industry staggering in the 1980s, it seized on services and declared 1987 'Visit Thailand year.' Following the financial meltdown in 1997, the previous government of Chuan Leekpai responded with the 'Amazing Thailand' promotional campaign. Facing a new economic downturn, the present government, under Thaksin Shinawatra, vowed to boost foreign exchange earnings from tourism by 50 billion baht (US$1.1 billion) in 2001. The target required that the country attracted an additional 1.9 million foreign visitors. Under the new plan, many thousands of hitherto undeveloped villages were earmarked for 'community-based ecotourism' projects. In the interim, a well-formulated conservation policy to counter the impact of increased visitor volume and spatial expansion of tourism was conspicuously absent. This suggests that the country's natural resources will further be sacrificed for short-term economic gains.

(2) 'Golfers' Dream—A Farmer's Nightmare

Since the late 1980s, golf has been aggressively promoted as a lucrative tourism business. Starting out from Thailand, the golf course boom spread into other Mekong countries causing immense environmental and social conflicts.

In the late 1980s and early 1990s, some 200 courses were built in Thailand. The construction of golf complexes—often involving other largescale developments such as hotels, residential houses, shopping centres, entertainment facilities, power plants, access roads and even airports—came under heavy attack for environmental reasons. Many of the projects were accused of encroaching on parkland and driving off farmers from their land.

Golf courses require large stretches of land and replace biodiversity-rich wilderness areas and fertile agricultural lands. Another major concern is the enormous waste of water resources for such projects. According to the Mahidol University in Bangkok, the turf of an 18-hole international standard golf course consumes up to

6,500 cubic metres of water per day which is equal to the daily household demand of 6,000 city residents or 60,000 villagers. While scarce water reserves are being diverted to keep the courses green, nearby communities are suffering due to the lack of drinking and irrigation water. In addition, the excessive application of chemical fertilisers and pesticides necessary to maintain the courses covered with foreign grass species threatens to pollute air, soil, and water, and create health risks for both wildlife and humans. Alarming reports were published in the Thai media about caddies and green-keepers affected by acute chemical poisoning—*e.g.*, headache, nausea, respiratory illnesses and skin diseases.

In the southern Lao province Champasak, Thai investors had plans to build a mega-resort project, including golf courses, hotels, casinos, a power station and an international airport, in a pristine area at the famous Lee Pee waterfalls on the Mekong River. Although the developers promoted the resort as an 'ecotourism' venture, it was met with resistance by Lao and Thai environmentalists as well as local villagers because it would have involved deforestation, ecological disruption of the fragile Mekong river system, displacement of villagers, and probably undesirable social and cultural changes in nearby communities. Consequently, due to increasing public protests and financial difficulties the controversial project was halted.

Vietnam has also built a number of golf courses to attract foreign tourists. Citizens protested when developers flattened a public forest in Thu Duc near Ho Chi Minh City for the construction of the Golf Vietnam Club. The Thai developers of the King's Island Golf Resort at the Dong Mo dam reservoir near Hanoi built a golf course at the edge of the lake below the reservoir's spill way level without considering rising water levels during the rainy season. During devastating floods in 1994, provincial officials allowed the release of large amounts of water from the reservoir to save the golf resort, which resulted in the destruction of the rice crops in neighbouring farming areas. Despite a 1995 governmental decree that prohibited converting more rice lands to other purposes, the South Korean conglomerate Daewoo received an investment licence to build a golf course on rice fields at Kim No village on the outskirts of Hanoi. Violence broke out at the construction site, when angry farmers, who had not been properly informed about the project, tried to stop an army unit from plowing up the land for the golf course.

In Cambodia, several golf course projects surfaced around Phnom Penh, near the Angkor Wat temple complex, and in Sihanoukville as part of the huge Naga Island casino resort proposed by a Malaysian company. For the construction of the Singapore-financed Cambodian Country Club at the Bang Ta Yab Lake outside of Phnom Penh, the developer wanted to drain a large stretch of marshland and remove more than 450 families who lived beside the lake (mostly fruit and vegetable growers). But the villagers refused to leave and protested to the authorities that, in turn, treated them as illegal squatters and refused to compensate them.

In military-ruled Burma as well, golf courses have sprung up at tourist sites, including luxury golf-plus-casino resorts such as the Golden Paradise Resort near Tachilek in the Golden Triangle and the Andaman Club on Thathay Kyun Island in the South. For the development of the Myanmar Golf Club in Rangoon, the army blockaded the site to scare off the people who had been living there for decades. When this failed, the government arrested one member of each family and sent them to jail. The remaining families were then moved against their will to a 'new town' far outside of the city.

(3) Cultural Heritage for Sale—The Case of Angkor Wat

In order to lure and entertain visitors, culture (as manifested in historical and religious sites, rituals, festivals, arts and crafts) has often been distorted beyond recognition in the process of being re-packaged as a tourist product. The famous twelfth century Angkor temple complex at Siam Reap—the most sacred site and national symbol of Cambodia—is a glaring example as to how cultural heritage is no longer for local people to celebrate, but increasingly commodities to lure foreign visitors.

With the Cambodian government aiming of 1 million foreigners a year to visit Angkor Wat, grave concerns have been raised that the temple area and its surroundings could be destroyed within a few years. In 1995, UNESCO's World Heritage Committee even threatened to remove Angkor from the list of protected sites because Cambodian authorities had not met the necessary requirements such as adopting a cultural preservation law to deter the theft and smuggling of antiquities. Thousands of invaluable artifacts have been stolen from the temple complex since it has opened to tourists. The government has vowed to take precautionary measures to ensure that protection zones at the historical and religious sites are respected. But this may not be enough to save Angkor due to inefficient bureaucracy, corruption and the absence of a functioning legislature and sufficient capacities to scrutinise, monitor and control projects.

Conservationists in and outside Cambodia were particularly appalled at the proposal for a US$20 million Angkor Wat High-tech sound-and-light show, saying it would turn the temples into a 'carnival-like attraction' or a 'Disney-like inane entertainment place.' In 1995, the Malaysian YTL company claimed it would promote 'the biggest and best cultural event of its kind in the world.' The plan was to stage up to four performances per night; in which the temple as well as selected bas-relief carvings on its inner walls would be illuminated in colourful lights and voices in different languages be heard from loudspeakers. In Thailand, where tourist shows at historical monuments have become commonplace, such activities have provoked debates regarding the extent to which old, fragile buildings are damaged.

The YTL company had also wanted to develop a 1095-hectare site near the northwestern temples into a tourism zone including several luxury hotels, golf courses, a commercial centre, a hospital and other facilities—a project which was expected to attract more than US$1 billion investment. In January 1996, even King Norodom Sihanouk voiced strong concern about the 'commercialisation' of Angkor and pressed for a review of YTL's plans for the light-and-sound show and hotel and the tourism complex in the area. However, since Prime Minister Hun Sen's bloody coup against the co-prime minister Prince Norodom Ranariddh in July 1997, which resulted in a dramatic tourism slump in Cambodia little has been heard regarding YTL's Angkor show and accompanying developments.

In an all-out effort to revive Cambodia's ruined tourism industry following the political turmoil, in 1999 the government adopted an open-skies policy to increase international flights to Siem Reap, the gateway to the Angkor temples. Additionally, it organised an extravagant 'Angkor 2000' millennium show. 'Tourism officials' hopes that the combination of direct flights from overseas and spectacular promotional events would make Angkor part of an international 'must-see' itinerary was being realised. In addition, the opening of new overland routes to Siem Reap from Thailand attracted more visitors and investors to the area and fuelled the construction of more tourism facilities around Angkor. As a result, renewed warnings of threats to the temples were been voiced in public, and there were growing worries that local people would be increasingly exposed to the effects of uncontrolled tourism.

(4) 'A Fascist Disneyland'—Tourism and Human Right in Burma

In 1996 the Burmese military government, which has been condemned by the international community because of its gross human rights violations, launched an ambitious tourism promotion campaign 'Visit Myanmar (Burma) Year.' The junta hoped to attract more than 2,50,000 foreign visitors to the country during 1996-97 to increase currency earnings and gain recognition in the international community after decades of isolation and a bloody military crackdown on the pro-democracy movement in 1988. While Burmese tourism authorities and the industry stepped up promotion to sell the country as the 'Golden Land,' critics increasingly delivered descriptions of Burma as a 'prison' for its citizens and a 'fascist Disneyland' for visitors.

Insisting that, in a country where people are denied basic rights, tourism cannot benefit that country, Burmese opposition groups and international human rights organisations have called for a tourism boycott to Burma. Democracy leader and Peace Nobel Prize laureate Aung San Suu Kyi has repeatedly urged foreign investors and tourists to stay away from the country until democratic reforms have been achieved. The argument is that the income generated through tourism helps to sustain the oppressive regime and is spent on buying weapons and expanding military action against its citizens. Since every foreign visitor entering the country has to purchase foreign exchange certificates equivalent to US$200, and many tourist facilities are state-owned, a considerable proportion of tourist dollars goes directly into the junta's coffers. In addition, members of the military run their own tourism-related businesses or have formed joint ventures with private companies to increase their personal wealth and economic power.

The close links between the development of the tourist industry and human rights abuses have been well documented by official agencies such as the United Nations Human Rights Commission, the International Labour Organisation (ILO) and Burmese and international civic groups.

Drawing on reports from Rangoon, Mandela, Pagan, Taunggyi, Maymo and other places earmarked for tourism development, it is estimated that tens of thousands of families have been forcefully moved from their homes and land to pave the way for hotels, resorts and tourism-related infrastructure. Most of the displaced people do not receive any compensation and have to resettle in areas which lack proper sanitation, electricity and water supply. Equally deplorable is the fact that ordinary people are forced into providing their labour to upgrade tourist sites and to build roads, railways and airports, in order to meet the increased transportation requirements for travel and tourism.

Burma's ethnic minorities, who have already suffered for decades under forced assimilation policies by the state, are now being lured away from their villages to serve as 'exotic' attractions in hotels or so-called 'model villages'. In addition, thousands of Burmese women and girls, many of them from ethnic groups, have become victims of a burgeoning domestic sex trade and are being trafficked to Thailand to work as prostitutes.

That 'Visit Myanmar Year' turned out a failure can be partly attributed to the success of the strong global movement against

Burma's tourism policies. Since 1997, tourist number has plummeted as a result of the Asian economic crisis and increasing international sanction against the country. During the fiscal year 1998–99, Burma attracted only 120,000 foreign visitors, less than half as many that the junta had expected when it announced its 1996 tourism campaign. Yet, Burmese officials remained optimistic and announced a new campaign aimed at increasing the number of tourists to Burma by ten times to 1 million in 2001!

Discussion: The Question of Sustainability

The above investigation on tourism policies and practices in the Mekong region reveals the vast gaps between 'sustainable tourism' as a theoretical ideal; what has been planned, and what has been actually achieved. The grim realities, as described in the various case studies, leave serious doubts as to whether tourism development can be propelled towards more sustainability in the long-term.

This is not to say that initiatives that have successfully managed to avoid major damage by fostering community based and environmentally sound tourist activities do not exist. It also should not be denied that some tourism companies have taken positive voluntary measures to mitigate impacts such as pollution. However, such 'success stories' are limited to a few micro-projects, and they have certainly not posed a real challenge to the *status quo* or considerably contributed to the redirection of the tourism industry as a whole.

A hard look at the overall situation leads us to the conclusion that the policies pursued by governments, national tourism authorities and supranational bodies, such as the Asian Development Bank, for the development of Mekong tourism have been those most suitable for promoting the industry rather than for the protection of the environment and the benefit of local communities. Put simply, in the words of Wall, tourism promotion in Asia over the recent years has consumed massive amounts of capital and has failed to create a sustainable product. It appears that there has been an implicit belief that tourism development is about the construction of high quality hotels and that, once these are in place, all else will follow.

Indeed, little has been done to develop effective mechanisms to monitor and control developments aimed at curbing environmental degradation, social and cultural erosion and economic marginalisation of the poor. Management plans, if there are any, are often ignored, and environmental, zoning and construction laws are not being properly enforced. Many critical tourism-related issues—such as corruption, social vices, encroachment of public lands and diversion of natural resources, displacement of local and indigenous communities, and political suppression and human rights abuses—are typically neglected by tourism policymakers and project managers. In the light of this, it is easy for critics to assert that 'sustainable tourism' in the Mekong region is little more than empty rhetoric and a public relations exercise to ward off public criticism.

What is it that makes it so difficult for tourism to deliver sustainable development, and why does there seem to be no prospect of significant positive change? Some explanations and aspects for further analysis will be provided in this last section.

Firstly, sustainability itself is not a fixed and agreed term, and thus is subject to interpretation. Associated with this are the various potential limitations of the concept that have been identified by various researchers. Wall (1997) notes that 'While sustainable tourism has drawn attention to the need to achieve a balance between business and environmental interests. . ., as a single-sector concept, it fails to acknowledge the intersectoral competition for resources, the resolution of which is crucial for sustainable development.' Addressing the issues of power and vested interest, Mowforth and Munt (1998) state that 'the principles of sustainable tourism are open to manipulation in the service of operators and others in the industry. That is not to say that the principles are not worthy of attention by all those in the industry; but it does suggest that the motives of those who apply them should also be scrutinised.' Finally, Wheeler (1997) contends, 'there are continual exhortations on the need to adopt a holistic approach to the subject of tourism development, planning and sustainability. . . . A truly holistic approach would be one that embraces realism. Sustainable tourism unfortunately fails, at the practical level, even to acknowledge it.'

In fact, the planning for 'sustainable tourism' in the Mekong region has largely remained a theoretical exercise without sufficiently taking into account the milieu in which tourism is evolving. Therefore, Majone's argument is worth savouring: 'A practical problem is not solved by offering a theoretical solution that does not take into consideration the limitations upon which the context imposes. Thus, it is quite misleading to employ ideal standards in evaluating or comparing alternative policy instruments; the standards must relate to the particular context in which the instruments are used. And because the context in which public policy is made includes values, norms, perception, and ideologies, technical considerations are insufficient as a criteria of choice.'

It is also important to note that the concept of 'sustainable tourism' is deeply rooted in Western environmentalism that often takes the form of 'enlightenment' and is dependent on achieving a certain level of prosperity and development. This, however, often appears to be at odds with the livelihood-based environmentalism in Southeast Asia and other parts of the Third World, where poor peasants and forest dwellers are struggling to defend and reclaim land and natural resources for economic and cultural survival. A better understanding to these contradictions may help to explain why so many ecotourism projects based on Western conservation ideals are resisted by local people and subsequently fail.

What is also often ignored is that globalisation has induced its own particular political dynamics in the region, which are to the detriment of the commitment to achieve sustainable development. In this context, Parnwell's study on how Mekong tourism has become part of the global race-to-the-bottom is instructive. Highlighting examples of human rights violations in Burma, sex tourism and the HIV/AIDS crisis in Thailand, and the environmental impacts of golf tourism in the region, he argues 'the impact of tourism depends crucially upon the ownership of regulatory power' and explains how transnational agencies and corporations work through and with influential local actors and institutions—what he calls 'conduits of capitalism.' His conclusion is that regulation for the global tourism industry is taking precedence over the regulation of its development.

As a result, local people, and especially the poor and marginalised, are exposed to greater political, social, economic and ecological insecurity.

Since in poor countries, especially, tourism's economic viability is seen as a prime criterion for sustainability, the old question of who actually benefits from tourism needs to be raised anew in the face of globalisation and liberalisation. Third World tourism is mainly driven by foreign industry interests, and the economic gains for destination countries are often greatly overestimated.

A 1990 study on Thailand by the Bangkok-based National Institute and Development Administration, for example, came up with disillusioning results. At least 60 per cent of tourism revenue, amounting to US$4 billion in 1989, had been lost to 'leakages,' being used for the import of goods and services and profits to foreign tourism corporations and other remittances. A new study prepared by UNCTAD on 'The Sustainability of International Tourism in Developing Countries' presents even more alarming findings. It emphasises that the economic, social and environmental sustainability to Third World countries' tourism industries is increasingly threatened by levels of financial 'leakages' that can easily reach 75 per cent, and escalating 'predatory practices and anti-competitive behaviour' of travel and tourism corporations based mainly in Europe and the United States. The UNCTAD report further points out that the combined impact of these factors undermines the economic viability of local enterprises and the ability of countries to allocate necessary resources for environmental protection and sustainable development. Under these conditions, the proclaimed goals of sustainable tourism to enhance local economic benefits and the preservation of natural and cultural resources are extremely difficult to achieve.

Important lessons regarding the fragility to the tourism industry can be learned from the Asian economic crisis that began in June 1997 with the financial meltdown in Thailand. It showed how much tourism is part of the fickle global economy, as well as being an industry that undergoes boom-and-bust cycles with serious consequences for the stability of national and regional economies.

There is little doubt that the inflationary tourism policies in the Mekong subregion in the early 1990s greatly contributed to the 1997 'crash.' During the era of the so-called 'bubble economy,' indiscriminate and unsustainable investments led to the rapid conversion of lands into opulent tourism resort complexes. With progressive economic liberalisation, the tourism, real estate and construction industries boomed in all Mekong countries, backed by local banks and global speculative capital.

In the immediate aftermath of the economic slump, Asian tourism markets almost collapsed. In Thailand, the currency devalued and major corporations—many of whom had expanded into Mekong's neighbouring countries—were exposed for having mismanaged their way into massive indebtedness. Many tourism developers went bankrupt or were forced to downsize their projects. In particular, golf course and resort businesses, which had become a new symbol of globalised leisure enhancing the tourist lifestyle in Southeast Asian societies, experienced a dramatic downturn.

Many tourism-related infrastructure projects initiated by regional cooperation initiatives, including those of the ADB, were put on hold, as resources were needed to strengthen Asian countries' financial systems. In Thailand, for example, the International Monetary Fund (IMF), the World Bank and the ADB granted a US$17 billion loan, which included a rigid Structural Adjustment Programme (SAP).

At that time, it had been suggested that in environmental terms at least, the Asian crisis could be a blessing in disguise. As a result of decreasing numbers of travellers, for example, airlines closed unprofitable routes, sold off aircrafts and cancelled orders for new aircrafts, and governments cut budgets for airport expansion and construction, which raised the prospect of less pollution and less damaging developments. Also, the malaise of rampant land grabs, park encroachments and environmental degradation in relation to tourism projects no longer seemed as threatening as before because Asian developers were cash-strapped

As it has turned out, however, Mekong tourism promoters not only returned to 'business as usual' but government in the region have made all-out efforts to compensate for the heavy debts, declining growth and decreasing foreign exchange reserves through even more rapacious resource extraction policies. A case in point is Thailand's present policy, aimed at turning every corner of the country into a tourist site and excessively boosting the number of tourists. Simultaneously, public and private investments in environmental programmes have significantly decreased because of the financial downturn.

Another question that should be asked is: Can tourism be sustainable in a region deeply affected by political instability, human rights problems and social-economic crisis? In the context of the preparations for 'Visit ASEAN Year 2002,' for example, tourism officials admitted that the event could be seriously hampered by political turmoil and social unrest in Southeast Asian nations but at the same time they tried to portray the problems as 'isolated incidents' to engender the notion of a 'carefree' holiday for consumers. As Richter notes:

> Scarcity, deprivation, inequality, remnants of colonialism and the proxy wars of the superpowers set the stage for random violence, ethnic conflict, revolution, and even hostage-taking. . . . The very underdevelopment that exacerbates the resolution of political demands and frustrates economic aspirations is a potential asset in attracting tourism. Thus we have a paradox: nations, which are veritable hellholes for most of their citizens, are sold as 'unspoilt paradises' to outsiders.

The concept of 'sustainable tourism' implies a high degree of public participation in the process, and public participation implies that local communities will have a degree of control over the tourism development process. However, the healthy-sounding words of 'local participation' and 'community control' often appear incredible and even bizarre, when applied to such destination countries as Burma, with no democracy or freedom for its own indigenous population. And 'Can a few corporate giants substitute for popular participation?' asks Shiva Kumar. As regards tourism planning and management, regional initiatives such as the ADV-led GMS tourism scheme rely too much on foreign consultants, who often have little knowledge of local situations, whereas 'the type of sub-regional projects so far proposal defy the spirit of local participation and sustainable development to which most donors and multilateral institutions commit themselves . . . .

The Mekong countries—particularly Burma, China, Vietnam and Laos—provide few opportunities for public participation in government decision-making. The exception to this generalisation is Thailand, which has relatively well-established civil rights and environmental movement, and a free press. Given the lack of individual freedom to speak out on development issues in the region, this task has by default fallen to a number of non-governmental organisations who, in turn, have sought to draw attention to the problems of tourism development, pressing for holistic and people-centred development policies that are not narrowly confined to tourism.

As outlined in the previous sections, major problems and conflicts have emerged because many rural and indigenous communities lost control of their land, natural and cultural resources and the political process as a result of 'top-down' tourism development. This being the case, one of the most urgent future tasks is to develop policies and tools to protect local people against uncontrolled and damaging tourism and to give them more power in developed and conservation projects in general.

A number of grassroots-oriented organisations are already working in this direction and have put forward proposals aimed at tackling fundamental problems in development and natural resource management. For instance, an alliance of civil society organisations and local community networks in Thailand have developed a 'People's Agenda' that calls for a comprehensive reform of government policies and urges policy-makers to take the following actions:

- assert sovereignty over natural resources and not to relinquish control to transnational;
- develop alternative economic systems based on the self-sufficiency of local communities, their use of natural resources and local knowledge systems;

- base its policies on natural resource management on a holistic view of natural and the diversity of natural ecosystems, cultures and knowledge systems;
- ensure local people's participation in drafting policies on the management of natural resources;
- guarantee, as well as strengthen, the rights of local communities to manage natural resources; and
- support the efforts of local community networks towards sustainable management of natural resources and local economic development.

Importantly, the previously outlined agenda calls for just and equitable land reform that favours small scale farming communities, and demands 'Foreign or Thai land-owners must be prevented from accumulating and controlling large areas of cultivable lands for speculative or non-farming purposes.' This proposal aims to resolve the escalating land conflicts flowing from speculative investments in hotels, golf resorts and other land-consuming tourism-related developments that involve the expropriation of village commons, agricultural lands and natural areas, and thus, increasing hardships for small scale farming communities.

At the present time, there is little evidence that 'bottom-up' development alternatives such as the 'People's Agenda,' based on the principles of economic equity, social justice, cultural integrity and ecological sustainability, are going heeded in tourism development planning, even though such grassroots-oriented proposals could be the key to root out the causes of problems. What are needed is more informed debate and public pressure to steer the tourism 'powers-that-be' towards a more holistic and people-centred approach and to persuade them to reorient their policies and practices accordingly. As Toe and Chang aptly note '. . . one should not underestimate the salience of local players in the global game. It is by them that the success or failure of tourism development is ultimately decided.'

5

Towards Sustainability: Examples from the UK Coast

The growth of tourism in the UK reflects the expansion of the industry worldwide. At the turn of the twentieth century the UK Government has calculated that British tourism:

- employs 1.75 million people in 125,000 businesses,
- has accounted for one in six of all new jobs created in the last ten years;
- is worth £53 billion a year; and
- brought 25.5 million overseas visitors to Britain in 1997

This well-developed tourism economy is heavily dependent on the environment, heritage, culture and the diversity of local landscapes and local communities.

At the Earth Summit in 1992, the UK Government made a commitment to Agenda 21, the global environmental and development 'blueprint.' Whilst there is little explicit reference to tourism within Agenda 21, much is relevant; and local government is perceived to have an important role to play in its delivery. Local authorities were urged to develop and adopt a Local Agenda 21—

a sustainable development strategy at the local level—by 1996. Local Agenda 21 guidance favours establishing partnerships with other sectors including businesses, voluntary organisations and community groups.

A national UK strategy for sustainability advocated inclusive social progress, effective environmental protection, prudent use of natural resources, and high and stable levels of economic development and employment. At the same time, consultation on how the UK might work towards sustainable tourism stressed the positive potential contribution of a sustainable approach, and sought views on key issues associated with meeting the economic and social requirements of people within a framework of resource conservation. Issues examined included transport, community benefits and management of visitor flows. In terms of planning imperatives, the consultation stated that sustainable tourism should be accessible, particularly to public transport and those cycling or on foot, and it should be based wherever possible on an existing well-located infrastructure.

Key outcomes of this exercise have been the publication of a new *UK Tourism Strategy and Sustainable Tourism Roundtable Guidance* for local authorities. The former announced the formation of a new national body for tourism with sustainability at the heart of its mission. The latter translated sustainable tourism into six guidelines on the basis that tourism should:

- integrate activity, long-term planning and partnership development;
- maintain and develop diversity;
- support local economies;
- use resources sustainably;
- involve local communities, stakeholders and the public; and
- research, share learning and experience.

Monitoring the delivery of sustainable tourism is, however, proving far more elusive than establishing guidelines. Miller (2001), in attempting to develop indicators for sustainable tourism, identified considerable expert disagreement over what constitutes sustainability and its conceptual boundaries.

This chapter focuses on coastal tourism. A series of case studies are presented as being reflective of the range of issues associated with the sustainable development of coastal tourism in the UK. The main contention of the chapter is that sustainable coastal tourism must focus on inherent strengths. For the rural coastal relate to the physical environment, for the urban coastline a unique heritage. Neither should be compromised by tourist activity

Coastal Tourism

The EU Demonstration Programme on Integrated Coastal Zone Management (ICZM) defined the coastal zone as 'a strip of land and sea of varying width depending on the nature of the environment and management needs. It seldom corresponds to existing administrative or planning units. The natural coastal systems and the areas in which human activities involve the use of coastal resources may therefore extend well beyond the limit of territorial waters and many kilometres inland.' This is particularly applicable to coastal tourism given that tourists are usually confined to a relatively narrow area, but the infrastructure need to support their activities including, for example, water and food supplies, transport access and accommodation for service staff, encompasses a much wider region.

ICZM has been defined as the 'process which brings all those involved in the development, management and use of the coast within a framework which facilitates the integration of their interests and responsibilities to achieve common objectives.' The framework should highlight and account for the interrelationship between individual issues and the management of the coast as a whole, since decision-making within one locality or one sectoral area is likely to impact upon others. In practice ICZM is still in its infancy and the intensification of use in the marine and coastal environments has become a significant issue only relatively recently. Johnson and Seabrooke (1996) suggested that new approaches and institutional support are needed to manage the marine and coastal environment effectively, efficiently, and above all in a manner which does not permit these environments to become degraded.

To date, relatively little work on marine tourism as a subject area in its own right has been undertaken. However, it is well documented that tourism has the potential to have a major impact on coastal areas. French (1997) stated that it is the intensity of tourism in a small unit area that differentiates it from other forms of development. Particularly acute negative environmental impacts are:

- over-exploitation of natural resources to satisfy tourist demand;
- loss of natural habitat and biodiversity as a result of resort development; and
- increased pollution, arising particularly from sewage effluent treatment and disposal problems.

Authors such as Cooper *et al.* (1998) have also highlighted positive and negative sociocultural impacts, such as changes in local culture, congestion and crime, which affect both hosts and guests. These too are very evident on the coast, often changing the cultural heritage of traditional fishing communities, for example.

The 20,000 kilometre UK coastline has a long history of tourism. The physical variety of the UK coast has often determined the type of tourist activity. Tidally dominated coasts are popular for water-based recreation; wave and wind dominated coasts for beach activities; and built up urban coasts have historically engineered sea front environments to 'accommodate' tourist facilities (including piers, beaches protected by sea defences, and mass tourism attractions). Increasingly, however, the UK coastline is being valued for environmental conservation, including many areas of international environmental sensitivity. To date, for example, 100 coastal and marine Special Protection Areas have been classified under the EC Birds Directive [Directive 79/409/EEC(OJ L103, 25.4.79) on the conservation of wild birds] and 35 marine Special Areas of Conservation have been identified under the EC Habitats Directive [Directive 92/43/EEC(OJ L206, 22.7.92) on the conservation of natural habitats and wild fauna and flora].

Strategic approaches are required to integrate environmental considerations within coastal tourism policies and plans. Detailed tourism planning is needed to identify issues liable to have an adverse effect on sustainability. This should focus on both physical and socio-economic aspects. Minimising the negative physical aspects of tourism can be achieved through the development of environmental risk assessments, determination of carrying capacities and identification of sustainability indicators. The latter include measurements of destination quality such as ecological impacts, energy efficiency and pollution control. Maximising the local economic and social benefits of tourism requires support for local economies including sustainable tourism related employment. It should also pay attention to local community involvement, cultural impacts and health issues. Dumashie (1997) suggested that coastal tourism planning should involve the correct definition and balancing of local specific assets and liabilities. Examples, which she cited, are given below:

Assets	*Liabilities*
Good scuba diving	Sand storms
Brisk sailing	Jellyfish infestations
Good fishing	Strong currents
Attractive moorings	Endemic diseases
Cruising trips	Sea fog
Exotic hinterland	
Historic towns	

Management tools and techniques are also important, including environmental assessment of tourism projects, management plans for destinations, environmental auditing and life-cycle assessment of destinations, visitor surveys, environmental monitoring, and promoting the role of best practice, training and education.

Many sustainable tourism principles are not new. They reflect, for example, values enshrined in the UK Town and Country Planning system. Nevertheless, British coastal tourism decision makers, and the communities involved, need to re-examine their tourism policies and practices. The following examples provide a 'snapshot' of work in hand.

Examples of Sustainable Coastal Tourism Thinking

Urban Coastal Regeneration—Redcar and Cleveland Borough Council

Many British seaside resorts, established in Victorian times, are suffering from a decaying infrastructure and outdated accommodation provision. They have been slow to adapt to structural change in holiday trends. Additional reasons for resort decline include improved personal mobility, insensitive architectural designs of the 1960s, lack of investment and environmental degradation. The principal trend is for more British people to take their main annual holiday abroad, using domestic seaside resorts for shorter breaks. Over a period of 20 years market share has declined significantly. Trips taken to the seaside, nights spent at the seaside and money used at the seaside, as recorded by the UK National Tourist Boards, have all continued to decline in the period 1991–1997.

Recognising the problem, reviews of resort issues by the English Tourist Board and Association of District Councils highlighted the need for a strategic approach, creation of an identifiable marketing image, partnership approaches and improved standards of visitor care.

Redcar and Cleveland Borough Council has been part of an EU-funded pilot study to demonstrate and evaluate the way forward in terms of developing successful resort regeneration action plans. This study comprised two European Network Projects that specifically examined the problems of resorts and the potential for achieving effective revitalisation with minimal funding. Lane summarised the findings of both projects and, in particular, concluded that resorts are a key function and element of the coastal zone. He also concluded that the suggested regeneration action plan methodology parallels the framework suggested for the preparation of Local Agenda 21 Action Plans. Essential elements within a five-year regeneration action plan rolling programme are considered to be:

- establishing a vision, the political will and overall commitment to regenerate;

- research to create a better understanding of visitor needs and tourism infrastructure;
- generation of ideas including those community groups and organisations and thus identifying the key issues such as zoning of development;
- formulation of policies, specific targetable actions and monitoring programmes; and
- provision of funding including attracting private sector investment.

The advantages of addressing this issue include reducing the potential for transformation and degradation of more natural sections of the coast. A central conclusion of the EU project was that 'existing resort areas provide a tremendous tourist resource and can handle, with minimum impact, substantial numbers of visitors.'

The UK Government is currently encouraging resorts to collect relevant baseline data and has tasked development agencies with raising the profile of resort regions to maximise chances of EU and other funding applications. The recently published strategy calls for 'imaginative, market led and sustainable regeneration programmes' and favours niche marketing, creating opportunities for all sectors of society, as one solution to reversing the economic decline.

As a result, many UK resorts are now working to establish a new identity and focus, investing in upgraded well-designed modern facilities, and striving to manage visitor flows in order to minimise seasonality. Action orientated plans, based on visitor survey information and involving resort communities, have been adopted. Environmental issues are acknowledged as paramount to resort action planning and the creation of a high quality, vibrant and effectively managed beach area continues to be seen as a key feature.

This example illustrates at least some elements of sustainability. It represents a holistic and integrated coastal tourism management policy, within which attempts are being made to balance the environmental needs of the destination with the investment returns required by the private sector. However, a sustainable vision will not be enough. Public funding is needed to build new attractions, renovate accommodation and improve public transport links. To be sustainable, redevelopment of this kind has a respect the scale, nature and character of each coastal resort, as well as reflecting the importance of the hinterland environment behind the beach. It must also tackle social inequity and deprivation.

Pump Priming—the Wales Tourist Board

Wales has a coastline of 1,200 kilometres, which includes the only UK coastal national park and a unique coastal heritage. The Wales Tourist Board's (WTB) role is to provide pump-priming finance, ideas and advice for tourism operators. WTB has embraced sustainable tourism in four key aims. These are to:

1. develop and market tourism in suitable ways which bring social and economic benefit to Wales;
2. offer high standards of product, quality and service;
3. support and promote Welsh culture and the Welsh language; and
4. protect and improve the environment, the natural beauty of the country and its buildings.

In this context sustainable tourism has been interpreted as being about developing and marketing local products and produce, minimising the environmental impacts of local visitor services and encouraging partnerships. Greenow (1999) highlighted the following examples of progressive steps, which illustrate how this is being achieved in Wales.

South Pembrokeshire Partnership for Action with Rural Communities (SPARC)

This rural development initiative has involved the local community in all aspects of tourism development. Thirty-seven villages have been involved working in the region of outstanding natural beauty around the Pembrokeshire Coast. National Park. SPARC has facilitated tourism planning based on initial assessments of communities. The result is a tourism programme that reflects shared community vision and therefore fosters local support. Green and heritage holiday packages using local cycle routes, public transport and luggage transfer services have been developed. This links with the efforts of 'greenways,' an attempt to integrate an improved environmental transport network, which includes footpaths, cycle routes and an enhanced public transport service. Wales currently has two new National Cycle Routes, which take advantage of traffic-calmed roads and off-road byways. The Landsker Borderlands Trail, for example, is one of several trails successfully promoted to the Dutch, German and UK markets, for which some 60 per cent of incoming travel is by train. Alternative holidays, based on environmental and cultural interpretation, are generating significant income for the local economy. This last point, reducing the leakage of tourism generated spending, is an important element of sustainable tourism. The aim is also to achieve a balance between the needs of the visitor, the destination and the host community.

'Greening your Business' manual . . .

The WTB have produced detailed guidelines for tourism operators, published in Welsh and English in the form of a manual. During 1998 manuals were sold commercially and issued to businesses securing WTB grants. As well as explaining the rationale for environmental action, the manual offers practical ideas for more environmentally friendly working practices whilst maintaining an attractive environment for tourists. Attention is given to:

- energy and water conservation (*e.g.*, low energy light bulbs, insulation, thermostat settings, preference to showers over baths);
- purchasing (*e.g.*, local supplies, organic food, minimum packaging);
- waste and recycling (*e.g.*, materials management, composting, sewage disposal);
- visitor environment (*e.g.*, access to gardens, home grown food, Welsh culture); and
- public transport opportunities.

In this instance encouraging the careful and efficient use of renewable and non-renewable resources and avoiding waste engenders sustainability.

Green Sea Partnership . . .

The Green Sea Partnership is a public and private sector partnership, which includes WTB and the major public utility Dwr Cymru/ Welsh Water, to co-ordinate and improve beach facilities and resources. Evidence of improvement in beach and coastal water quality has been the increase, from two in 1995 to 13 in 1998, in the number of beaches gaining European Blue Flag awards. A Rural Beach Awards category has also been established for small, quiet beaches without recreation infrastructure. The Partnership aims to survey 120 of these smaller beaches annually. Public and private sector partnerships of this type can encourage sustainable tourism, not least by raising awareness of business benefits associated with good environmental practice and through the adoption of 'environmental management tools.' An informed public is more likely to visit and respect beaches demonstrating high environmental standards.

Managing Visitor Flows—The National Trust

The National Trust for Places of Historic Interest or Outstanding Natural Beauty is the UK's largest voluntary conservation organisation, with a membership of 22 million and an annual income of over £83 million. Whilst the National Trust is a charity, and thus perhaps not strictly a tourist operator, the organisation channels income from visitors into maintaining and enhancing landscapes and local culture. It is also an example of a voluntary organisation whose core activity relates to sustainable development.

In 1965 the National Trust launched Enterprise Neptune, a campaign to save the coast both for and from the public, which aimed to:

- acquire unspoilt coastline for permanent preservation and public access;

- alert people to the increasing pressures and threats to the coast; and
- raise funds for the purchase of unspoilt coastline.

Over 35 years this initiative, now renamed the Neptune Coastline Campaign, has been spectacularly successful, raising over £33 million enabling the acquisition and management of 960 (or 1 in 6) kilometres of the coastline of England, Wales and Northern Ireland (Scotland has its own National Trust). This has included a wide diversity of coastal sites with different problems. Among them are a number of extremely popular sites where visitor management strategies and techniques have been implemented to promote sustainable tourism, at the same time respecting and integrating biodiversity conservation objectives. The National Trust encourages people to enjoy their coastal properties whilst at the same time promoting good stewardship. An educational programme entitled the 'Coastal Guardianship Scheme' involves local people with their coastal properties. Three of these coastal 'honey pot' sites are described below.

The Farne Islands

The Farne Islands off the north-east coast of England are home to large colonies of nesting seabirds. Yearly visitor numbers rose from around 3,000 in the 1970s to over 50,000 in the mid-1980s, enthused by media wildlife coverage. The National Trust determined to limit visitor number and negotiated permits with local boat owners. The result is that now only eight boats have permits. They transport a maximum of 3,000 visitors per day to one location for a one-hour visit; walkways are roped and boardwalks prescribed where needed; and nesting birds take little notice of the 'ecotourists.' Over time this approach has worked well, achieving improvements in both habitat conservation and the quality of the visitor experience. Visitors can observe seabirds at close quarters, they understand that their visit is not damaging the environment, and local boat owners benefit. In this case sustainable tourism is clearly about 'demand regulation,' but it is also an example of tourist activity respecting the intrinsic value of the coastal environment and not prejudicing its long–term future.

Kynance Cove

The National Trust acquired Kynance Cove in Cornwall in 1935. The beauty spot attracts in excess of 1,00,000 visitors annually. In 1986 land adjacent to Kynance Cove was acquired. Prior to this the headland had been in private ownership and visitor facilities comprised a number of *'ad hoc'* buildings, a large car park and eroding cliff top footpaths. The National Trust has demolished unsightly structures, incorporated a new car park within the landscape, restored and re-routed footpath access. Visitor income now funds environmental conservation.

Studland Bay

Studland Bay, at the western extremity of Poole Harbour in Dorset, is possibly the UK's most popular rural coastal destination, attracting up to 12,50,000 visitors each year. The National Trust owns a six-kilometre stretch of beach together with an immediate hinterland of dunes, marshland and lowland heathland of high nature conservation importance. Facilities, including a visitor centre, car parks and raised boardwalks, have been developed to accommodate large numbers at peak times. The visitor management strategy concentrates visitors in an area with high carrying capacity and protects fragile areas.

Heritage Interpretation—Dorset County Council

Much of the county of Dorset's coastline is designated as Heritage Coast and much, including Studland Bay, is owned and managed by the National Trust. The Jurassic Coast Project is a three-year feasibility study that aims to address the fact that 80 per cent of the region's tourism income is derived from 20 per cent of visitors. The coastline, which is highly regarded for its landscapes, rural beaches and pretty villages, attracts large numbers of day visitors but these visits are restricted to a relatively short summer season.

A solution to improving the local standard of living, whilst simultaneously protecting the environment, is based on the region's outstanding geological heritage. The coastline reveals a complete Jurassic sequence from east to west (150 million years of geological history) and incorporates the largest coastal mudflow in Europe. Rapidly eroding cliffs are the source of world famous landforms such as Old Harry Rocks, Durdle Door and Lulworth Cove; spectacular fossils, including recent new dinosaur finds; and evidence of a fossil forest and dinosaur footprints. With the support of European Union funding, Dorset County Council is attempting to use this unique earth science legacy to generate 'out of season' tourist interest, extend visitor stay time and maximise economic benefit to the region. The initiative epitomises sustainable tourism principles and reflects the dynamic nature of coastal conservation. In the past the conservation ethos has been preservationist. The Jurassic Coast Project will enhance opportunities for visitors to enjoy landscapes, ecology and local character and culture by maximising the potential of information and communication technology to explain the dynamic nature of coastal processes. Niche tourism will feed on, rather than diminish, local distinctiveness and diversity. In this instance geology provides the linking theme and is the basis for a World Heritage Site bid for this stretch of coastline.

For Dorset County Council an investment in heritage interpretation provides the key to a more sustainable approach. Working papers have highlighted new educational initiatives, an interpretation strategy and a marketing approach. This supports the viewpoint that tourism can be a positive activity with the potential to benefit resident communities, visitors and the destination. It also complements the work of Purbeck Heritage, a partnership of councils, landowners and conservation bodies, together with Purbeck District Council's management plan to promote more sustainable forms of tourism in the region. Tourism planners in Dorset hope that special interest breaks, employing local experts, will benefit accommodation providers at times when tourist numbers are low. Geo-tourism potential can be realised in the 'shoulder' months when coastal scenery is more dramatic and when fossils uncovered by winter storms are more likely to be found. Dorset Tourism Data Project statistics indicate that visitors drive around the coast to a series of short stay places of interest. The Jurassic Coast Project aims to provide these visitors and educational groups with sufficient interest in one place.

A site-specific focus for a more sustainable approach is Portland and the Isle of Purbeck. This 'island,' linked to the coastline by a causeway, has been dominated by the quarrying industry and by its role as a strategic military base. Quarrying for Portland stone continues but the Royal Navy is relocating its operation. A Quarry Park, incorporating both working and abandoned quarries, is proposed as a tourist and educational alternative. A combination of unique geographic position, wildlife interest, spectacular views, cultural interest associated with buildings, structures and artefacts (including a sculpture park) made from Portland stone provide a 'one stop shop.' The focus on cultural heritage will create opportunities for local people to share their knowledge and enthusiasm with visitors. Increasing the participation of local people and communities in this way is indicative of an emphasis on social responsibility, another key element of sustainability.

Conclusions

Sustainable tourism acknowledges the fundamental link between long-term planning, conserving the environment, economic gain and profitability from tourism operations, and social equity. Appropriate tourism policy and planning on a holistic and integrated basis is required by all stakeholders. Success is based upon:

- maintaining and improving levels of natural capital stock through accurate and objective assessment of resources;
- controls to observe carrying capacities;
- an adequate investment in resource efficient ancillary services;
- opportunities for all parties to contribute particularly local involvement;
- raising public understanding and promoting intergenerational equity;

- effective environmental policies, tourism management plans, and equitable economic and employment benefits; and
- long-term monitoring, assessment and feedback.

In a review for Tourism Concern, Leslie and Muir argued that take up of Local Agenda 21 within local authority tourism strategies in the UK was poorly funded and left significant room for improvement. Like so much of the hype generated by the sustainable development concept, much remains on paper rather than in practice. Since then the UK Government has at least attempted to raise the profile of sustainable tourism but politicians are still searching for easily measurable ways to ensure that tourism practice does not contravene sustainable development principles.

The UK coastline is an example of a natural resource that has been used and abused for many years. The case studies selected suggest that increased voluntary efforts to deliver sustainable tourism are currently being made. In these cases the management of tourist activities has the potential to re-shape the industry. A number of urban coastal resorts, such as Redcar and Cleveland, are planning positive regeneration projects. In hitherto unspoilt rural areas a sustainable approach is being developed on a partnership basis by government agencies, voluntary organisations and local groups.

However, the case studies chosen also illustrate the absence of a coherent and comprehensive approach to the sustainable management of the UK coastal zone. Local government is leading much of the drive towards sustainable tourism at the coast and sustainability is not yet a mainstream concern for most private sector providers. Consequently, sustainable development ideals and actions have little prominence in the most popular coastal destinations such as Blackpool, Skegness or Newquay.

It could also be argued that the majority of UK tourists themselves give little thought to sustainability. Mass tourism along parts of the southern Spanish coast represents the antithesis of sustainability. However, some 1.5 million UK tourists holiday each year in the Spanish resort of Benidorm on the Costa Blanca, and on the Catalan coast, which includes the Costa Brava. Some environmentalists consider that pollution and over-development, much associated with tourism in these areas, have pushed their coastal ecology to a 'critical point'

All the examples cited are attempting to combine protection or enhancement of the coastal environment, economic wellbeing of coastal communities, a healthy distinctive local culture, and maximum visitor satisfaction. Nevertheless, it also clear that better networks are needed to both apply the results of research and to promote and share good practice. Sustainability must be fully recognised as part of coastal tourism policy and decision-making, and its success or otherwise needs to be measured, judged and broadcast. Ultimately, in order to realise quantifiable gains, a proactive approach from the tourist industry will be required, along with a more responsible approach by tourists to their interactions with the natural and built environment.

6

Steps Towards Sustainability Monitoring

In response to more than a decade of unrestrained growth, British Columbia's tourism industry is under intense scrutiny as regards its impact on the community and environment. As a consequence several of the province's industry and community leaders have begun developing strategies that are designed to focus tourism development in more sustainable directions. A critical component of such strategies involves developing and implementing monitoring processes that provide credible measures of how well tourism is doing in achieving sustainability goals. In this regard, one of the province's most significant tourism destination communities has taken the lead in the development and use of a comprehensive monitoring programme. Over the past six years, the Resort Municipality of Whistler has been systematically monitoring its progress towards its identified growth management goals. This case study examines this monitoring programme with a view to determining its performance against recommended sustainability assessment processes.

The Role of Indicators

To assess progress towards more sustainable forms of tourism, there is a need for relevant monitoring systems. Ideally, these systems should focus on assessing the extent to which existing best practices in tourism are aligned with, and help to achieve, core sustainability goals. In this regard, sustainability monitoring should be focused on examining progress towards reaching a combination of ecological, social and economic imperatives.

Indicators can be used to measure progress towards sustainability goals, and when tracked over time, can also help identify trends in the condition of a phenomenon that has significance beyond that of the measurement itself. For example, an indicator of transportation modes into a resort area could help to measure progress towards the achievement of non-renewable resource consumption and air-pollution goals. Ideally indicators used for assessing progress in the sustainability area should:

- be selected on the basis of input received from a broad base of stakeholders;
- be designed to meet the varying informational needs of these different audiences;
- include objective measurements (*e.g.*, biophysical measure-ments such as water quality parameters);
- include subjective measurements (*e.g.*, stakeholder perceptions and attitudes); and
- signal where necessary the need for comprehensive studies of more complex relationships.

Developing Indicators

Researchers and practitioners have identified several processes for developing sustainability indicators. Many of these processes have commonalties that appear to be applicable in the context of tourism communities. These include visioning, scoping, determining indicator selection criteria, selecting indicators, analysing and reporting findings, and soliciting feedback.

Visioning

A variety of methods have been suggested for collecting the information needed to create a truly community based vision of an area's sustainability goals. These methods include using a combination of town hall meetings; workshop brainstorming sessions; livingroom focus groups; questionnaire surveys; key informant or expert consultations; open house meetings and displays; and public meeting panel discussions to identify the set of goals to be achieved through tourism development activities.

Scoping

This second step involves establishing the scope of the monitoring programme. By creating an understanding of the role and benefits that a credible monitoring programme can create for existing tourism organisations and other community stakeholder groups, practical decisions need to be made with regard to:

- scope (politically, spatially, temporally); what development issues should be addressed; and
- how to determine what relevant data might be collected and by which methods within a monitoring programme.

By collaborating with tourism operators, local businesses, community and environmental groups (as well as neighbouring communities), and regional and provincial governments, a priority set of issues can be identified for monitoring. A balance must be found between providing an all-encompassing set of indicators and the fiscal realities of collecting, assimilating and interpreting the information. This scoping exercise should address not only the range of issues and indicators to be measured, but also the spatial scale and range of audience to whom the findings of the monitoring programme's activities should be targeted. For instance, depending on the situation, the target audience might range from primarily community decision-makers, to business operators, to provincial government policy-makers. All of these stakeholders may play distinct but important roles in influencing the way in which development unfolds in tourism areas. In each of these cases, it may be necessary to establish different levels of indicator reporting sophistication (*e.g.*, range and number of indicators) in order to ensure relevance to each group.

Choosing An Indicator Framework

Indicator frameworks provide systematic means of structuring the identification and selection of relevant subjects/issues to be monitored. A variety of different frameworks have been developed for application in varying sustainability monitoring contexts. Generally they fall into five broad categories.

Domain-based frameworks

Domain-based frameworks can address a variety of tourism performance issues. These include not only economic performance indicators commonly associated with tourism industry activity, but also critical social and ecological concerns, which often provide the underlying foundation for much of tourism's potential sustainability. Depending on the circumstances, specific domain-based indicators can be selected or accentuated in order to emphasise critical linkages between environment, economy and society. However, domain-based frameworks do not necessarily link indicators directly with specific management goals, thereby reducing their overall utility for monitoring progress towards sustainability.

Goal-based frameworks

Goal-based frameworks focus on identifying indicators that can respond directly to sustainability goals. In a tourism community context, these goals may include such concerns as: achieving specified resident satisfaction levels; maintaining targeted visitor traffic levels; providing a specified supply of affordable employee housing; and protecting a specified amount of sensitive habitat for conservation purposes. Such frameworks are particularly useful in systematically reducing the number of indicators required for monitoring purposes. This makes monitoring and assessment processes more manageable in many cases. The overriding weakness with goal-based frameworks is that the separateness of each indicator reduces opportunities for identifying important inter-relationships between various factors affecting tourism's sustainability. For example, goals such as resident housing and environmental conservation can be pursued in isolation and may ultimately conflict with one another, but would not necessarily be considered within a goal-based indicator framework.

Sectoral frameworks

Sectoral indicator frameworks respond to the needs and structures of existing institutional organisations. Typically, they focus on issues linked to the functions and focus of specific management groups. From a tourism community perspective, sectoral frameworks might describe indicators of existing land use, housing, transportation, recreation, and social infrastructure service conditions. Over time, the indicators measured in such frameworks can be useful in assessing the impact of specific management responses to particular development issues. However, this type of compartmentalised approach to monitoring tends to reduce the range of ecological, economic and social influences on specific issues.

Issue-based frameworks

Issue-based frameworks address specific 'hot' topics such as traffic congestion, resident housing, and wildlife conservation. While valuable in short-term management contexts, these issue-based frameworks often take the systematic rationale needed to provide a comprehensive perspective on issues having longer-term sustainability implications.

Causal frameworks

Causal frameworks provide indicators that are useful in systematically measuring existing conditions, stresses and responses related to sustainability issues. The strength of these frameworks lies in their ability to determine potential causal relationships between economic, social and environmental factors. Causal frameworks provide indicators that normally address issues concerning what is actually happening (*i.e.*, state or condition indicators); why is it happening (*i.e.*, pressure or stress indiçators); and how management is addressing the pressure (*i.e.*, response indicators);

Within causal frameworks, performance can be evaluated by comparing indicator trends with set management goals. For example, in the case of a mountain stream within a tourism community, an indicator of its condition (state) might be the water flow during low tourism visitation periods compared to its flow during peak visitor traffic periods. Per capita water consumption rates (pressure) might be used as an indicator of what current stresses are placed on the stream by visitors. Finally, a set of water conservation practices (response) might be used to assess the extent to which various water restriction targets are feasible under varying management regimes. While a very systematic approach to monitoring, past applications of causal frameworks have typically failed to address the within-domain interactions of essential components and structures within ecosystems.

An integrated pressure–state–response indicator option

Combining the strengths of the previously described indicator frameworks can provide more comprehensive alternatives for sustainability monitoring. For instance, a domain-based approach combined with a pressure–state–response (PSR) system can offer a valuable integrated approach to systematically assessing tourism's progress towards a variety of interrelated goals. Most importantly, this approach facilitates the integration of policy initiatives across sustainability imperative domains. In essence, this means that the relationship between various management response indicators within one domain can be examined in the context of a state and pressure measure in another domain. For example, an economic response indicator of increased resort promotion can be compared with environmental pressure indicators such as habitat area lost.

Identifying Potential Indicators

Numerous indicators are available to tourism and community planners. These include lists of 'core indicators' derived from general community and regional planning contexts, as well as those designed specifically for tourism. Many of these lists can be obtained on the World Wide Web. For example, the sustainable Communities Network (http://www.sustainable.org) and Hart Environmental Data (http://www.subjectmatters.com/indicators) offer extensive indicator lists. Additional potential indicators can also be developed which respond to unique local sustainability goals. Community visioning may provide guidance concerning what these potential indicators might be.

Selecting Indicators

Selecting a final set of key indicators from the long list of measurement options can occur in a number of different ways. For example, practical considerations such as data affordability and availability issues, as well as the perceived relevance to potential users, may help determine the overall appropriateness of specific indicators. Each indicator must be judged according to its appropriateness on a predetermined scale. Since conflicts may arise amongst decision-makers concerning the relative importance of each selection criteria, there may be a need to weight the relative importance of each factor. Once a set of preferred indicators has been identified, a review determining the completeness and balance of the final set can be carried out to ensure that all the major dimensions of sustainability are represented. The final set should be modified as required. The PSR matrix, in particular, is a useful framework for making this final assessment of completeness.

Analysing and Reporting Progress towards Sustainability

After indicator measures have been collected, the findings should be analysed. Ideally this entails not only reporting individual indicator values, but also establishing historical trends in specific indicator values, and identifying progress towards specific sustainability goals. Furthermore, where feasible, cause and effect relationships between pressure, state, and response indicators should be attempted. This analysis phase may prove difficult as different opinions may exist about the meaning of indicator trends relative to sustainability goals. For example, the number of building permits issued in a tourism community may indicate economic prosperity to some, while it may indicate an unacceptably high rate of natural land conversion to those more interested in environmental preservation.

The reporting of the findings emanating from the collection process should be tailored to the target audience. For instance, a brief summary report with key indicators should be appropriate for the general public who may not be concerned with a lot of complex information. In contrast, a more detailed report can be prepared for technical staff. This information can also be made available to interested stakeholder groups upon request. Ideally, these reports should include:

- explanations of the significance of each indicator itself and an explanation of the types of value judgements incorporated into its selection;
- assessments of past trends and anticipated future trends in indicator values relative to established target levels;
- graphical representation of indicator trends; and
- where feasible, a discussion of linkages between indicators.

Soliciting Feedback

Soliciting feedback to indicator reports should also be actively pursued. This can be encouraged in a variety of ways. For example, it might be useful to seek feedback via television, radio and print media, as well as public meetings, public surveys and focus groups. All of these techniques can help to refine indicator selection, measurement, and interpretation processes. In any reporting process, an acceptable level of relevant indicator information must be displayed in order to maintain stakeholder interest and at the same time the effort expended must not unduly tax personnel and financial resources of paid and volunteer data collectors in the community.

Responses to requests for indicator refinement by the lead agency must also be evident or the process runs the risk of stakeholder alienation.

The Whistler Case Study

Tourism development in general, and mountain community tourism in particular, are often characterised by a combination of conflicting demands placed on what are frequently limited and fragile natural resources. Growth management is an approach to planning that seeks to capture the benefits of growth while mitigating its negative consequences. Typically, this involves implementing a range of management strategies including: protecting community sense of place; managing tourism related impacts; identifying community commercial and social priorities; securing stakeholder commitment to specific programme initiatives; and managing tourism demand towards specific community objectives. Such growth management strategies rely heavily on data in the form of indicators to chart progress towards more desirable and sustainable future conditions.

Since 1994, the Resort municipality of Whistler has undertaken several initiatives to develop and implement a monitoring system that has several sustainability components. Originally enacted in 1976 to encourage compact development and discourage sprawl, Whistler's growth management strategy has expanded to become an integral part of the community's Comprehensive Development Plan and a focus for the municipality's monitoring programme. The growth management strategy addresses issues encountered in many mountain tourism communities (*e.g.*, alpine environmental protection, land use sprawl control, affordable housing provision, community and tourism infrastructure development). In this respect, Whistler's growth management strategy is both innovative and exemplary. However, what distinguishes Whistler's growth management/initiative programme from those of other tourism destinations is its monitoring programme. Initiated in 1994, the monitoring programme is intended to communicate information to the community on how the destination has been changing. This monitoring information is also used to encourage community discussion concerning the selection of appropriate strategies for managing future development and growth.

Many of the elements in Whistler's monitoring programme are consistent with the recommended steps for sustainability reporting described previously. The monitoring initiative addresses the influence of various growth pressures on: resident quality of life; natural environment quality; and affordable housing.

Whistler's Visioning Process

Whistler's Comprehensive Development Plan outlines several general goals that relate to an evolving 'vision' for the resort municipality. The vision is about the values, scope and priorities that should drive management activities in the resort municipality. The formal goals are to:

- enhance the Whistler experience, for those who live in Whistler and for those who visit and use the resort, by balancing the environmental, economic and social needs of the community and the resort;
- continue to move towards environmental sustainability, by fostering and participating in a wide range of environmental partnerships and management initiatives associated with maintaining the high quality of the area's natural and built environments;
- build a stronger resort community, recognising that this is an important aspect of enhancing the resort; and
- achieve financial sustainability by implementing a range of public and private sector partnerships designed to support the community economy, as well as introducing a range of innovative and cost effective methods of delivering municipal services.

The community's monitoring programme has been designed to measure change in the community as a result of growth. However, it should be noted that there has been no explicit consideration of the principles of 'sustainability' (except perhaps in an intuitive context related to 'sense of place' criteria) in establishing the appropriateness of the types and level of growth taking place in the community.

Scoping the Whistler Monitoring Programme

The target aùdience for the Whistler monitoring programme has been loosely defined as 'community stakeholders.' These stakeholders consist primarily of permanent residents and second homeowners. Stakeholder participation has, on the whole, occurred via annual 'town hall' meetings, community attitude surveyes carried out in 1991 and 1995, livingroom focus groups in 1995, and a variety of community visioning processes since 1997 (*e.g.*, community workshops, stakeholder group meetings, workbook surveys).The geographic scope of the monitoring programme was decided by the municipal planning department. It roughly matches the institutional boundaries of the municipality. Little explicit consideration has been given to temporal aspects of the data or indicator trends. Also, no limits have been placed on the amount of data, or number of indicators, reported. Reconsideration is currently being given to the scope of issues addressed by the monitoring programme.

The Use of a Sectoral/Issue-based Indicator Framework

The data and indicators reported in Whistler's monitoring report have been presented in sectorally based categories related to: development; social characteristics; environment; community facilities and infrastructure; economic benefits; transportation; and resident and visitor satisfaction. This framework was selected by municipal planners in response to the institutional structures that existed at the time of the first monitoring programme. In 1995, the indicator framework was modified to incorporate both sectoral and issue-based indicators. While using the same basic framework, some of its content since then has been modified by the community's municipal planners in response to issues raised by stakeholders in the annual town hall meetings. For example, monitoring information dealing with the state of undeveloped valley lands, natural habitat conditions in protected areas, as well as air and water quality have been added in response to resident requests.

Indicator Selection Criteria

No explicitly defined criteria were used in selecting the indicators employed in the monitoring programme. However, municipal planning department representatives did use indicators that were readily available (*i.e.*, existing data or easily measured); displayed historical or trend information; were comparable with existing data and information; and responded to stakeholder issues expressed at town hall meetings.

Indicators Selected

The Whistler monitoring programme reports information concerning all the indicators it selects. While no overriding 'key indicators' are highlighted, the most recent monitoring report includes over 80 indicators organised within a predominantly sectoral framework. Perhaps half of these indicators address some aspect of the concept of sustainability's environmental and economic imperatives.

Monitoring Programme Reporting

The resort municipality publishes its annual community and resort monitoring report for public distribution and reading. Typically, the report includes measurements associated with all of the selected indicators identified. In addition, an annual bulletin with summary indicator information is published. This document is intended to inform a wide audience and stimulate informed stakeholder debate about growth management issues.

Each year these reports, and an additional display of information, are viewed and discussed at an annual open house and town hall meeting. At the 1996 meeting, for example, formal discussion was encouraged around issues related to the most beneficial types of future land development, key growth management concerns, environmental programme issues, and future monitoring programme refinements. Similarly, in 1997, that focus of the town hall meeting was on seeking input to the municipality's vision statement that was in the initial phases of development at that time. It was expected that this vision statement would eventually drive the focus on future monitoring efforts. Subsequent public meetings (1998-2001) have focused on specific sustainability issues, such as housing, transportation and watershed management.

The perspectives presented at these town hall meetings are considered by the municipal officials and staff when creating new policies and selecting new indicators for subsequent years. For example, transportation and affordable housing issues identified at previous town hall meetings have become municipal programme and monitoring priorities in subsequent years.

Notwithstanding these initiatives, gaining an appropriate level and representation of attendance at these reporting sessions is a continuing challenge. Efforts are under way to solicit feedback from younger people, as well as social and environmental stakeholder groups in the community, in order to create a more inclusive perspective concerning the impact of growth on Whistler

Assessment of Indicator Performance

To date, Whistler has not placed a strong emphasis on linking each of its reported indicators to specific community sustainability goals. As a result it is difficult to assess whether or not the indicators have been effective in measuring progress towards these goals. Consequently, the municipality has not conducted a formal assessment of the effectiveness of the data or its indicators. However, there is some informal recognition that there is a need to create a more systematic linkage between the goals and the reported indicators. This recognition has emerged as the monitoring programme has matured, and as the demand for the inclusion of additional performance indicators has expanded.

Conclusions

In many ways, the Whistler Community and Resort Monitoring Programme represents an exemplary initiative. However, its full potential is not being achieved because the focus of the programme has been primarily to monitor various dimensions of growth impact as opposed to measuring progress towards the development of a more sustainable tourism community. As a consequence, there has been no clearly articulated vision, goals or process for the development of sustainability indicators (Table 1).

However, the Whistler monitoring programme is still valuable for a number of reasons. First, it was implemented with the clear objective of maximising the involvement of a broad group of community stakeholders concerned about a wide range of tourism growth issues. In this context, stakeholders were invited to participate in community decision-making associated with such issues as community size, housing options, and environmental management. Second, the monitoring programme has also assembled a considerable amount of valuable information that is important for enlightened discussion by community stakeholders concerned about these and other growth related matters.

Despite the programme's best intent there is a growing sense that much of the monitoring information collected is not generating the type of discussion on pressing and emerging issues that it was intended to create. Possible explanations for this perceived apathy might include the lack of any well-accepted indicators of progress towards the resort community vision or goals, as well as the lack of a resort community vision that reflects the principles and objectives of sustainability. Only in recent times has a comprehensive programme been implemented to develop a vision of Whistler that clearly identifies a set of consensus-based community priorities and directions. The community's local government believes that this visioning process and its subsequent vision statement will help to refocus, refine and improve the community's monitoring programme. In addition, the municipality has been developing a comprehensive Whistler Environmental Strategy (1999 to the present) along with a complementary community-wide sustainability awareness and engagement process called 'Whistler. It's Our Nature.' Early observations indicate that these initiatives will stimulate the creation of a more focused monitoring process in the community.

Beyond the need for more explicit sustainability goal-indicator linkages, there are also lessons to be learned with respect to the

Table 1
Comparison of sustainability reporting and Whistler growth management monitoring programme processes.

Model sustainability reporting process criteria		*Whistler growth management monitoring process*
1	2	3
1. Identification of Community Sustainability Goals	Use a multi-method visioning process (*e.g.*, town hall meetings, workshops, focus groups, open houses, surveys) to establish broad-based stakeholder defined sustainability goals.	Used goals established in Comprehensive Development Plan as proxy for community vision; input for CDP goals derived from limited number of open houses, information meetings and public hearings. No distinct focus on sustainability goals were identified.
2. Scoping	Determine target audience Consider spatial and temporal bounds Include institutional partners Establish relevant number of indicators.	Community stakeholders were target audience. Spatial boundaries were lands within municipal jurisdiction. Number of indicators and institutional partners were not established prior to implementation.
3. Choose Indicator Framework	Select combinational framework which maximises ability of indicators to assess progress towards sustainability (*e.g.*, PSR matrix/domain).	Used a combination of sectoral/issue-based frameworks. Framework evolved in response to departmental organisation and issues raised by stakeholders.
4. Define Selection Criteria	Select indicator criteria-based on community values and sustainability	Formal selection criteria not explicitly defined; informal criteria were

	2	3
	goals determined through stakeholder involvement.	related to data availability, affordability and relationship to growth management.
5. Identify Potential Indicators	Use existing listings of indicators as base; use stakeholder input to refine listings to potentially viable sustainability indicators.	Used existing local and regional data which appeared to match best with stakeholder issues.
6. Select Final Indicators	Apply indicator framework and selection criteria to 'long list' and select a final set of indicators.	No formal process was used to select indicator list. No formal attempt was made to refine indicator listings based on sustainability or growth management goals.
7. Analyse Indicator Results	Compare indicator values and trends to specific indicator target levels based on community sustainability goals.	No analysis with the exception of 'bad unit ceiling' and a few other indicators such as air quality was undertaken. Few established targets were used to assess indicator values against goals.
8. Report Indicator Results	Report a relevant number of indicators to the target audience and solicit feedback.	Annual monitoring reports and discussions at town hall meeting were used to present findings and solicit feedback.
9. Assess Indicator Performance	Assess indicator measurement relevance to identifying progress toward established sustainability goals.	No specific goals for most indicators were established; therefore, no assessment of indicator performance was conducted.

development process for assessing tourism monitoring programmes. In particular, emphasis should be placed on:

- involving a broad and inclusive group of stakeholders in the scoping exercise, as well as the selection of relevant indicators tailored to the target audience;
- developing partnerships with other local and regional institutions affected by tourism so as to increase cost efficiency and comprehensiveness in the collection of relevant data;
- using less compartmentalised indicator frameworks (*e.g.*, pressure–state–response) which facilitate the reporting of tourism's growth on various dimensions of ecosystem integrity and natural resource consumption;
- using comprehensive indicator lists developed elsewhere to help guide the selection of relevant indicators which cover critical sustainability issues; and
- reporting the monitored indicator data to community stakeholders via a variety of communication mediums (*e.g.*, monitoring reports, summary bulletins, newspaper articles) prior to and after public meeting presentation and workshops.

Whistler's monitoring programme was designed to disseminate relevant information to community stakeholders and stimulate enlightened discussion on future growth management decisions. However, it has only been partially successful indicator achieving this goal. Whistler and other resort communities considering the implementation of such programmes can enhance the appropriateness and relevance of their activities by taking a more sustainable community-oriented approach to their monitoring programme. When taken together, Whistler's recent efforts, specifically: the generation of a vision statement for the area; the creation of a comprehensive environmental strategy; and the development of a sustainability awareness communication programme, point to the area being in a much better position in the near future to implement a truly focused and effective monitoring programme.

7

Uganda's Bwindi Impenetrable National Park

In Sub-Saharan Africa, a human population in need of development is increasing the pressure of the region's natural resources. This pressure is particularly strong around national parks and preserves where people have been denied access to the resources viewed as necessary for development. As a result, park managers often find themselves in competition with local people. The traditional response to this competition has been the strict enforcement of park boundaries and the adoption of an 'us versus them' mentally. However, alternative responses are now proving more successful. Innovative and creative approaches to park management are resolving this conflict by simultaneously conserving park resources while stimulating local development. This case study explores how one national park in Uganda has been able to meet the challenge of conservation and development through the introduction of sustainable tourism.

Historical Background

Uganda is an equatorial nation of 241,139 km^2 (the size of Great

Britain) located in East Africa. It shares its eastern border with Kenya, to the south are Lake Victoria and Tanzania, to the west Rwanda and the Democratic Republic of the Congo (DRC), and to the north Sudan. Located within these borders is an amazing diversity of flora, fauna and human cultures. This diversity is reflected in the land itself. The glacier-capped Rwenzori Mountains crown the western horizon and rise from lush tropical forests. The western Rift Valley and its dry savannah contrast with the papyrus swamps and wetlands in the Lake Victoria basin where the source of the Nile River can be found. And finally, in the east, the sun rises from behind the 4,321 metre Mount Elgon, an extinct volcano. Owing to this diversity, by the late 1960s Uganda was home to a prosperous tourism industry. At that time, roughly 1,00,000 tourists visited Uganda each year and made tourism the country's fourth largest earner of foreign exchange. Unfortunately, the young industry came to an abrupt end in the early 1970s due to political unrest marked by the rule of dictator Idi Amin. Also at this time, much of the wildlife which contributed to the country's popularity was killed for food and trade.

It was not until the mid-1980s that the political climate in Uganda improved and the rule of law was restored. By 1986, a stable government was in place and free elections were forthcoming. By the late 1980s, conditions in the country allowed for re-investment in Uganda's once lucrative tourism industry. However, the loss of charismatic wildlife in previously popular safari parks such as Queen Elizabeth and Murchison Falls precluded them from competing with similar tourism attractions in neighbouring Tanzania and Kenya. This called for a redirection of Uganda's tourism industry away from East Africa's famed big game safaries. By capitalising on a global interest in tropical forests, Uganda's new tourism development strategy highlighted its own forest resources as tourist attractions, and by so doing, created a niche for itself in the competitive East African market. The keystone of Uganda's new tourism industry became the Bwindi Impenetrable National Park.

Bwindi Impenetrable National Park

Bwindi Impenetrable National Park (BINP) is located in south-western Uganda. It is situated in three separate countries and surrounded by eighteen parishes. To the south of the park, the Virunga volcanoes dominate the landscape while to the north the Rwenzori Mountains can be seen. BINP also shares a border with the DRC and covers 330 km^2 of extremely rugged topography ranging from 1,160 metres to 2,607 metres in elevation. As such, it is one of only a few forests in Africa with lowland, medium altitude and montane ecosystems in continuum. This makes BINP the most biologically diverse forest in East Africa. It is from this dense, often impassable forest, that Bwindi takes its name. In fact, Bwindi means 'a difficult place to pass through' in the local Rukiga language. Within the park are more than 220 species of trees, 100 species of ferns, 340 species of birds, 200 species of butterflies, and 120 species of mammals, including half of the world's population of the highly endangered mountain gorilla (approximately 310). In order to ensure the preservation of this ecologically important area, the forest was gazetted a national park in 1991 and a World Heritage site in 1994.

Despite its global significance, the creation of BINP was not well received among the local people. BINP is situated within three districts in Uganda: Kisoro, Kabale and Rukungeri. At the time of the park's creation in 1991, Uganda's average rural population density was 85 people/km^2. However, Kisoro district averaged 302 people/km^2 and Kabale district 246 people/km^2 making them the first and third most densely populated districts in the country, respectively. There was, and still is, tremendous human pressure on the land around BINP. Therefore, the creation of the park meant that valuable resources would be taken from a needy local population. Historically, the forest was an important source of revenue. Local people used it for timber, gold mining, hunting, and the harvesting of fruits, medicinal herbs and a variety of other forest products. Removing these resources from the local economy created hostility towards the park and its staff. Indicative of this hostility was the penchant for referring to the early park staff as baboons, an animal loathed for its destructive crop-raiding tendencies.

As this brief history of the park shows, the creation of BINP was accompanied by two major challenges: the conservation of a globally significant ecosystem that includes one of the world's most endangered mammals (the mountain gorilla), and creating development opportunities for local people who lost access to valuable resources. These challenges are typical of many parks throughout Sub-Saharan Africa.

BINP's Tourism Development Plan

The park's inception in 1991 was accompanied by hundreds of thousands of US dollars of loans and grants targeting conservation. In addition, technical assistance from a variety of non-governmental organisations (NGOs) was provided. However, it was recognised that the long-term ability of BINP to meet the dual challenge of conservation and development depended on its own revenue-generating capacity. More importantly, local people needed justification for the park's conservation, justification in the form of direct economic benefits. Towards this end, tourism was seen as the best option. Prior experience with mountain gorilla tourism in Rwanda and the DRC proved that it could be a profitable enterprise; in 1989, gorilla tourism in Rwanda was the nation's third largest earner of foreign exchange. Unfortunately, both Rwanda's and the DRC's success with gorilla tourism was short-lived due to political turmoil and war. As a result, Uganda was positioned to become the world's premier mountain gorilla tourism destination. To capitalise on the opportunity, a tourism management plan was developed for BINP in 1992 and implementation began soon after.

BINP's tourism development plan was guided by five principles:

1. tourism activity must support conservation, not be an end in itself, and be sustainable in the sense that it does not act to disturb or destroy the very attractions it is based upon,
2. local participation in tourism activities will be encouraged wherever possible and relevant, including policy matters and practical economic involvement;
3. tourism development will take place in a context of

environmental awareness, through guidance on appropriate ways to develop accommodation and other tourist facilities;

4. policy and planning will leave room for adaptation and experiment under the guidance of a steering committee; and
5. private sector activity will be encouraged under appropriate supervision and monopoly interests avoided.

It was believed that by following these guidelines, the objective of encouraging tourism focused on viewing mountain gorillas and other natural attractions in BINP could be tailored to meet the park's dual objectives on conservation and development. Specifically, the plan intended tourism to be sustainable, conservation-oriented, beneficial and empowering for local people, environmentally aware and economically viable.

From the viewpoint of environmental sustainability and conservation, the health of the mountain gorillas was the highest priority. Because gorilla tourism throughout Africa was relatively new, its long-term effects on the animals had not been thoroughly studied. Therefore, it had to be approached cautiously. The underlying concern was the genetic similarity between gorillas and humans. Because of this similarity, it was believed that gorillas might be susceptible to diseases brought into the park by tourists. In order to reduce these risks, the tourism development plan allowed only two groups of gorillas to be habituated to the presence of humans. This represented less than 10 per cent of BINP's gorilla population. The two groups would be monitored daily and their health compared to a control group which was not habituated. Furthermore, the plan devised strict guidelines to regulate tourist/gorilla interaction. Specifically, each habituated group would be visited by only six tourists a day for a period of only 1 hour, visitors had to maintain a distance of at least 5 metres from the gorillas at all times, and children under 15 as well as sick adults would not be permitted to participate. These controls would be rigorously enforced. In addition, educating the tourists and increasing their environmental awareness prior to viewing the gorillas was made a fundamental component of the tourism operation.

With regard to the spread of tourism's benefits into the local community, the creation of economic activity was the most obvious route. Local people would be hired as guides, trackers and porters. Park infrastructure development would use local materials and labour. Tourist accommodation would provide employment opportunities and linkages to the local economy through the sale of food and handicrafts. However, considering the large number of people living around the park, such avenues would provide a relatively small number of benefits. Therefore, more innovative approaches were needed, approaches which would spread benefits throughout the distant communities and reach large numbers of people. Revenue sharing and community extension work were two such ideas. Revenue from gorilla tourism was expected to be high and the plan called for 10 per cent of this revenue to remain in local communities for development projects. Furthermore, local people would be given the power to determine which projects would be funded from the shared money. BINP would also employ 'community conservation rangers' whose job would be to provide expertise in community development and conservation projects. Education was proposed to link all such development activities to tourism revenue generated by the park. In this way, the plan proposed tourism as the means to produce community-wide benefits and improve local attitudes about the park.

Evaluating BINP's Tourism Development Plan

It has been almost 10 years since the development of BINP's tourism plan and during this time well over 20,000 visitors have trekked to the gorillas. The cost of visiting the gorillas more than tripled from 80 US dollars in 1993 to 250 US dollars in 2001, yet the park continued to operate near capacity. BINP has become the largest source of revenue for the Uganda Wildlife Authority (the parastatal body which manages Uganda's national parks and reserves). Profits from BINP fund protected area management throughout the country. From an economic standpoint, gorilla tourism at BINP is clearly a success for the Uganda Wildlife Authority (UWA). This, however, was never really in doubt. Instead, the necessary question to evaluate is whether gorilla tourism is a sustainable approach to conservation and community development around BINP.

Before BINP was gazetted a national park in 1991, the largest threat to the mountain gorilla's survival was destruction of habitat due to logging. Without a doubt, creation of the park has ended these activities and the gorilla's habitat is secure. In addition, the daily presence of rangers, guides and tourists in the forest has been credited with curbing these and other illegal activities such as the hunting and trapping of wildlife. The gorilla population is now increasing, with exact numbers to be obtained in a census planned for 2002. The two habituated groups of gorillas experiencing tourism are living normally and reproducing at regular rates, suggesting that tourism is low impact and unobtrusive. Based on this success, and coupled with the demand for gorilla tourism, BINP began habituating a third group of gorillas with the intention of having them ready for tourism by late 2001. However, unexpected events with these newly habituated gorillas have challenged the sustainability of gorilla tourism in BINP. It is these challenges to which this case study now turns.

This third group of habituated gorillas, called Nkuringo groups, has become so accustomed to the presence of humans that they now spend the majority of their time outside the park near the village of Ntungamo located in Nteko parish. They often feed and sleep on people's farms. Among the problems that this has created is a health risk to both gorilla and human populations due to prolonged and close contact with each other. As if to confirm these fears, the gorillas recently contracted scabies and it is believed that the infection was spread through human contact. A subsequent survey conducted in Ntungamo village found that four of the 182 households were infected with scabies as well. It was also found that this village has very low latrine coverage and no rubbish pits. The habituated gorillas frequenting this village have most likely been exposed to human waste and rubbish. On the bright side, UWA was very quick to act on behalf of both gorilla and community health. The gorillas were immediately treated for scabies and a full recovery is expected. In the village, educational sessions were organised focusing on health and hygiene, and a village clean-up day was organised during which over 200 kg of garbage was collected. Fortunately, the daily monitoring of the habituated gorillas diagnosed the problem early, and before it could become more serious. In hindsight, the Nkuringo gorilla experience may be for the best. In addition to raising awareness about disease transmission, it has taught park managers that communities living around the park can have as much of an impact on the gorilla's health as the tourists who visit the gorillas on a daily basis. This lesson emphasises the importance of community education and co-operation for the sustainability of gorilla tourism.

In addition to these conservation lessons, events currently taking place in Ntungamo village reveal how tourism can improve community attitudes about BINP. Before the advent of tourism, gorillas entering onto community land would be chased deep into the forest or worse. The situation in Ntungamo is quite different. The community is not only tolerating gorillas in the farms but is actually excited to have them there. The reason for the change of attitude is clear. The community has already started clearing a spot for the construction of a tourist campground and hostel. They are anxious for tourism to begin as they see economic benefits flowing from visitation. This situation also provides BINP with a unique opportunity to expand its partnership with local people. This will be necessary if tourists are to view gorillas when they cross from the park onto community land. In Ntungamo, innovative approaches are needed in order to keep tourism sustainable and under the control of BINP's professional managers.

That a community would equate gorillas with economic opportunity is not unprecedented at BINP. Until the habituation of the Nkuringo group, all gorillas trekking originated in the village of Buhoma in Mkono parish at the park's main entrance. From Buhoma, tourists would trek to one of the two habituated groups of gorillas. Community members from Buhoma and the surrounding parish, with the assistance of a US Peace Corps Volunteer, formed a co-operative and secured a grant from the United States Agency for International Development (USAID) enabling them to construct simple tourist accommodation. The result was the Buhoma

Community Campground. This co-operative is governed by a committee composed of a representative from each village in the parish. The committee decides how profits will be spent. All profits go towards local development in the parish and completed projects include the construction of three schools and two medical clinics. The organisational success of the Buhoma campground was offered as a model for the village of Ntungamo which was planning tourism with the Nkuringo gorillas. A potential problem with the Buhoma site is that outside interests have bought land in the area and are now competing for the tourist dollar. As a result, some tourism revenue is leaking out of the community.

Clearly, tourism has had an impact on the parishes surrounding the park which receive tourists, but even with the addition of the Nkuringo gorillas, tourism directly benefited only two parishes. This left sixteen parishes in need of tourism's benefits. Spreading tourism's benefits to these other parishes has been the task of BINP's revenue sharing and community conservation programmes. To date, tourism revenue sharing has generated nearly half a million US dollars and funded over twenty community-based projects including road construction, schools and medical clinics. Although change has been slow, it seems these developments may be improving local attitudes towards the park.

CARE (an international conservation-oriented NGO) conducted a longitudinal study from 1997 to 1999 to measure changes in community attitudes towards the park. The survey was based on two random samples of adults living around the park. The sample was stratified to ensure that every parish was represented. The 1997 survey included baseline socio-economic data. Three different indicators were found to be significant in characterising the wealth of the respondents: ownership of a house roofed with iron sheets (versus grass thatching); ownership of a radio; and land ownership versus land needs. It was found that 65 % of the respondents had iron sheets for roofing; 34 per cent owned a radio; and 7 per cent believed that they had more than enough land (32 % just enough, 41 % not enough, 20 % had no land at all). Comparison with a follow-up survey completed in 1999 shows only slight changes, where it was found that 71 per cent of respondents had iron sheets for roofing; 37 per cent owned a radio; and 3 per cent believed they had more than enough land (22 % just enough, 53 % not enough, 21 % had no land at all). Thus, some indicators of wealth had slightly increased but so had the apparent need for more land. The significant of this information is that it shows that the majority of individuals around the park, despite the hundreds of thousands of dollars tourists spend there annually, have not experienced a significant economic windfall. Considering this, the investigation focused on whether attitudes about the park were remaining negative.

In 1997, people were first asked to state the costs and benefits of living near the park, and which was greater. Overall, 68 per cent felt the costs were greater. Secondly, the people were asked if they felt better off or worse off than other people with the same quantity and quality of farmland who happened to live further from the park. Overall, 77 per cent said they were worse off. Finally, people were asked about the distribution of park benefits between local people and potential outside beneficiaries (tourists, other Ugandans, UWA staff, the international community, etc.). Overall, 51 per cent of respondents felt that outsiders received more benefits, 39 per cent felt local people received more benefits, and 10 per cent felt it was an equal split. These same questions were again asked in 1999 and revealed a positive change. By 1999, the percentage of people surveyed who felt that the costs of living near the park outweighed the benefits dropped to 46 per cent; those who felt that they were worse off than other people with the same quantity and quality of farmland who happened to live further from the park dropped to 49 per cent; and finally, those who felt that outsiders received more benefits dropped to 44 per cent, while the percentage who felt that local people received more benefits rose to 45 per cent, and only 6 per cent felt it was an equal split. This suggests that an improvement in attitude towards the park is taking place. Because socio-economic data does not indicate a clear increase in individual wealth, it may be that this change in attitude in correlated with the park's many community-based development projects. The success of tourism revenues in funding these projects and improving livelihoods may be responsible for the improving attitudes towards the park. This is an area for future research. However, this much is clear, judging by the competition for resources in Africa, community support is essential in natural resource-based tourism is to be sustainable.

At this point in BINP's history, nearly 10 years after the development of its first tourism plan, the park can claim success. The dual objectives of conservation and development are slowly but surely being met. The mountain gorilla is now safely protected and tourism has contributed to its conservation. Likewise, tourism has provided community-wide benefits such as improved roads, education and health care, which will hopefully lay the groundwork for greater future development. However, 10 years is not a true test of a project's sustainability. Many challenges still exist as human populations around the park continue to increase. An interesting finding in the CARE survey of local people is that they are beginning to want more individual benefits from the park and tourism. Additional future challenges to the park's success may come from across its international border with the DRC, where instability has already proven disruptive to BINP's tourism.

In early March 1999, a small force of rebels operating out of the war torn DRC crossed into BINP and murdered eight tourists and one park warden. During the ensuing mêlée, much of the parks infrastructure, including the community campground, was pillaged, burnt and otherwise destroyed. It was a horrible human tragedy and seemed likely to cripple Uganda's growing tourism industry and scar the country's favourable international image. In fact, this was the rebels' stated goal. However, what actually followed was quite to the contrary. The people around the park mobilised themselves to improve security in the area. The military formed a new partnership with the park staff and deployed troops along the border. The Ugandan President guaranteed the future security of all tourists. The community campground was rebuilt and there are plans to expand it, and most importantly, the tourists returned. The park is once again operating at near full capacity and has had no further incidents. The resilience of the park to this tragedy would not have been possible without the full co-operation of local people, park staff, the Ugandan government and the international community. This may be the strongest indication yet of the sustainability of BINP's tourism development plan.

Conclusions

Despite its ecological uniqueness, Bwindi Impenetrable National Park is typical of parks throughout Sub-Saharan Africa. The challenge that these parks face is the conservation of valuable and sometimes endangered natural resources in the face of a growing human population. The lesson that must be learned is that the continued existence of these parks depends on their ability to extend the benefits of conservation to local people. In the case of BINP, tourism has proven to be a sustainable method of achieving this goal. However, the model that BINP presents should be studied carefully before it is implemented at other parks and protected areas. Firstly, BINP still relies heavily on donor support despite the lucrative tourism there. This is because BINP is not independent of the UWA and its profits must fund protected area management throughout the country. Therefore, the national context within which a tourism development plan is proposed should not be overlooked, as it can affect its sustainability. Secondly, revenue sharing may not be feasible in parks without a high dollar attraction, such as that derived from mountain gorillas. If not planned wisely, revenue sharing can quickly raise the hopes of rural people and leave them unfulfilled. Thirdly, the expert and regular monitoring of natural resources is essential if tourism is to be sustained. The importance of this was demonstrated by BINP's quick and effective response to a scabies outbreak among the Nkuringo gorilla group. Having said this, the most critical point remains. Regardless of the circumstances, innovative and creative ideas are necessary for spreading tourism's benefits throughout rural communities. Traditional economic channels employ only a small portion of local people. Furthermore, local enterprise can sometimes be out-competed by more capital laden external investors. As this case study of BINP demonstrates, keeping tourism's benefits local is the key to sustainability.

8

Con Dao National Park: Convicts and Conservation

The phenomenal growth of tourism experienced by the East Asia-Pacific region in the 1990s, almost double the world average, has played a formative role in reuniting and empowering countries long fragmented by conflict and genocide. Stimulated by an increase in disposable income and leisure time, greater political stability and openness, and aggressive promotional campaigns, tourism is further credited by proponents with discouraging unsustainable practices in environmentally sensitive areas, while simultaneously creating greater opportunities for women and ethnic minorities to participate in the development process. As a result, governments throughout the region are now busy positioning their countries as 'authentic' destinations for visitors interested in local culture and nature.

However, not every country or community in Asia will succeed as a tourist attraction, and those that do may discover that the economic benefits are less consequential than the social costs, as residents find their governments more intrusive and traditional practices rendered inauthentic for tourists' consumption. Further obstacles include the tarnished image associated with the sex tourism industry in Bangkok; continued land-ownership and use conflicts; ill-defined jurisdictional roles and boundaries; ethnic and gender disparities; a lack of coordination between participating agencies; and a preference for large-scale development projects financed by international donors.

The challenges of balancing such development with environmental conservation—and the possibilities offered by tourism in reconnecting an area long defined by its history of conflict, through expanded networks of travel and communication—are the topic of this case study on Con Dao National Park (CDNP) in southern Vietnam. Both strategy and process, the practices initiated on Con Dao, establish a framework for community and government leaders who truly wish to:

- successfully market and maintain protected areas as destinations for both foreign and domestic visitors;
- create long-term funding support for environmental conservation and education projects that unite both parks and communities;
- generate and support economically and socially sustainable employment opportunities; and
- develop meaningful, collaborative partnerships among the diverse stakeholders.

In achieving these goals, initiatives on Con Dao seek to balance tourism's promised benefits with the ecological significance and fragility of the park's marine and terrestrial environments. They also seek to affirm conservation as the primary function of a national park, yet acknowledge the economic needs of the destination community. In a landscape where resources are finite and political conditions uncertain, the proposed pathways additionally serve to reinforce the belief that sustainable tourism requires a sustainable community.

Background

Hoping to capitalise on the boom experienced by its neighbours in the Greater Mekong Subregion (Cambodia, the Lao PDR, Myanmar, Thailand, and China's Yunnan Province), Vietnam has recently taken significant steps to attract more international visitors. Plans to introduce single pricing at 21 tourist sites to remove the distinction between local Vietnamese and foreign travellers are expected to facilitate visitation and investment, as are simplified visa regulations and greater access by foreign airlines. In addition, 16 cities and provinces have established local tourism promotion boards, and, in 1999, the Vietnam National Administration of Tourism opened an overseas information bureau in France. Added to these efforts, the Vietnam State Steering Board, spent approximately 14.5 billion Vietnamese dong (US $ 1.05 million) in 1999–2000 on marketing the country's tourist attractions through a website and electronic newspaper.

Not unexpectedly, given the pro-tourism stance of the Vietnamese government, there are now many innovative developments taking place in the tourism area, amongst which is the Asian Development Bank's (ADB) funded eco-tourism 'demonstration project' administered by the World Wide Fund (WWF) of Nature-Indochina Programme in Con Dao National Park. The site of an infamous prison complex originally constructed by the French in the late 1800s, and subsequently used by the US-backed Saigon government during the 1960s to intern political prisoners, the island supports a diversity of flora and fauna that are increasingly prized for both their ecological and their economic value.

Con Dao

Located in the South Sea, approximately 160 km offshore from the 'Nine Dragons' of the Mekong Delta, the Con Dao archipelago consists of Con Dao island and thirteen smaller islets. Con Dao town, with a population of approximately 4,200 persons—75 per cent of whom are military—is the district capital and headquarters for the national park. Considered both a political and an ecological 'hot spot,' CNDP is the second largest marine park in Vietnam with 14,000 ha of marine habitats and 5998 ha of protected terrestrial forest land.

The park's waters are famed for their ecological diversity, including endangered green sea turtles and dugongs, and reputedly, the highest collection of giant clams in the world. The island's forests are equally noteworthy, including nearly 300 species of trees, of which forty-four are found nowhere else in Vietnam. Because of this high level of biodiversity and the presumed potential for eco-tourism, Con Dao is designated an 'Area of Highest Regional Priority' in the World Bank's Global System of Marine Protected Areas.

The ADB-funded demonstration project in CNDP joins other similar experimental programmes in southern Cambodia and central Vietnam. The intent of these 'eco-tourism demonstration' projects is to showcase practical options for sustainable managing tourism in protected areas throughout Asia, by identifying processes and methodologies that prove effective in conserving resources and stimulating greater public participation. Based on input received from the participating agencies, marine eco-tourism was made a central component of CNDP's *Five Year Management and Investment Plans* (1998–2004), as was the need to encourage and subsidise local tourism enterprises owned by community members, women, and ethnic minorities.

Destination Analysis

As a prelude to discussing in detail sustainable tourism initiatives on Con Dao it is useful to examine in more detail its attractions and infrastructure base along with the challenges it currently faces. It is essential to keep in mind, however, that tourism development on Con Dao is still at the incubation stage, and both preferences and practices continue to evolve as managers and residents assess the impacts and changing dynamics of travel to the islands.

Attractions

The islands of CNDP have remained relatively undisturbed until recently, due largely to their use as a prison, distance from the Vietnamese mainland, and their mountainous interiors. As a result, forestry researchers from the government-planning institute in Ho Chi Minh city have discovered a diverse range of mammals and marine life throughout the archipelago, including deer mice, the rare black squirrel, macaque monkeys, the first giant water monitor lizard, butterfly and parrot fish, giant clams, and the endangered green sea turtle and dugong. Seasonal migrations of dolphins and 'black whales' (*Prodelphinus malayensis*) have also been recorded in the coastal waters of the park by staff from the Institute of Oceanography in Nha Trang and the Institute for Environment and Sustainable Development at Hong Kong University of Science and Technology. Indeed, studies conducted between 1997 and 1999 suggest that the islands may offer the highest species diversity of corals found in Vietnam—and the most attractive in all of Vietnam in terms of eco-tourism.

Though the natural environment is certainly the primary attraction—and concern—of park managers, it is difficult to discuss development options for CNDP without consideration of the cultural attractions that exist on park and district land. Among the most significant is the prison complex initially constructed by the French colonial government in 1862. Further expanded by the former Saigon government in the late 1950s, the prison includes the infamous 'Tiger Cages,' where many of Vietnam's current leaders were held captive until the fall of South Vietnam in 1975. A national cemetery situated nearby includes the grave sites of 2,000 former prisoners, including Le Hong Phong and Vo Thi Sau, both nationalists executed by the French, yet still revered by the Vietnamese people.

Con Dao town also contains a historic district centrally located adjacent to the prison complex and hotels. Among the remaining buildings are the former head office and residence of the local governors, constructed in 1873. Considered to be the oldest surviving building on the island and unchanged for nearly 126 years, it now houses the Con Dao Museum. Also in close proximity to the prison complex is number of other culturally significant sites, including Pier 914 (the name refers to the number of prisoners who died during its construction); the remains of a road and stone wall near Cau Ma Thien Lanh, where nearly 350 prisoners reportedly died under the French; the Phi Yen temple; and the Salt Prison. Some smaller sites are located inside the park itself, including a small house on Hon Cau where Pham Van Dong was held prisoner, and the ruins of a former French plantation.

Infrastructure

At present, entry to Con Dao for most non-resident is available only by boat or helicopter, weather permitting. A Malaysian-owned cruise ship from Star Cruise Lines used to stop at Con Dao each week while en route to Thailand. However, the port calls (which began in October 1999) ceased in September 2000, reportedly because the passenger load averaged only 200 persons per sailing, or less than a third of the ship's total capacity. Consequently, visits to Con Dao remain relatively small in number, totalling less than 3,000 annually, based on admission records maintained by the park office and the Con Dao Historical Museum. However, ADB and Phuong reported that the airstrip was to be upgraded to accommodate 70-passenger prop jets operated by Vietnam Airlines, and that there were plans to launch an inter-island ferry from Singapore.

Additional data provided by the two largest government tour operators, Saigontourist and Vietnam Tourism, indicated that 46 per cent of the international eco-tourists who visited southern Vietnam—and by extension, Con Dao—were from East Asia, followed by Europe (7%), North America (3%), and Australia/New Zealand (1%). Most arrived during the brief dry season (April–July) when travel by boat was more reliable and less expensive for Vietnamese nationals, and as a result some overuse of certain sites was occurring during this period. Nonetheless, the Ba Ria-Vung Tau provincial government, in whose domain CDNP lies, was still very much concerned with expanding visitation. Indeed, with this goal in mind it announced plans to launch a high-speed boat in early 2002, capable of carrying 200 passengers from the provincial capital of Vung Tau to Con Dao island in only 7 hours. A similar boat would transport guests to a South Korean planned, 500-room hotel complex located near the park entrance. The provincial government was also planning to extend the 27-km paved road connecting the airport, Con Dao town, and Ben Dam port to eventually encircle the entire island. This construction project was designed to facilitate access to the west coast for day visits and for security patrols by the military.

Challenges

While efforts at growing visitation may benefit the local economy, they might also cause extensive environmental degradation. Soil erosion and the dumping of hazardous waste now threaten sensitive marine environments along the route of the road construction, as do the harvesting of coral, and turtles for sale and consumption. The runway expansion and a proposed casino on the island's north will result in the elimination of significant bird-nesting sites and possible contamination of nearby beaches. The potential shortage of drinking water in the future (particularly during the dry season) is also an environmental challenge that must be addressed.

On Hon Bay Canh, where the park maintains a guard station, fresh water must be supplied by boat—though the Vice-Minister of the Ministry of Agriculture and Rural Development (2000) had voiced his intention to construct water cisterns on each of the islands where ranger stations exists. In Con Dao district, the local government is already constructing additional storage facilities, prompted by the accelerated loss of the island's fresh water and mangrove systems to development. It is therefore not surprising that it is worried about the consequences should the island's population total 15,000 inhabitants by the year 2010, as projected in the district's Master Plan (1992). Given the limited amount of land available outside the park, such growth would also place tremendous pressure on the island's other resources and likely necessitate further importation of food and supplies by helicopter or ship.

Limited electrical capacity on Con Dao is also a major issue and inconvenience, since the system is shut down completely between midnight and 0600 hours except for hotels and private homes with generators. Waste disposal presents an additional challenge. Although garbage is collected by the district, most residences rely on poorly-maintained septic systems for human waste, and solid waste is frequently abandoned on parklands contiguous to inhabited areas.

Additional stopovers by cruise ships, as some tour operators desire, and the completion of a proposed hotel where the island's only source of fresh water now lies, will only generate further conflict between businesses who favour 'high-end' tourism and proponents of smaller scale attractions and facilities. In addition to the total number of visitors, the current mix of Asian and Western tourists has other implications for the nature and level of development on Con Dao in terms of facilities, attractions, and activities. Interviews with self-labelled Asian and Western eco-tourists in 1999–2000, for example, established that many Asian visitors to Con Dao prefer to travel in large groups and to stay in local hotels or other comfortable accommodations. The majority of Westerns eco-tourists, however, opt to travel independently and seek more direct, cross-cultural experiences and a simpler standard of accommodation. Information concerning such experiences and services, nonetheless, is not easily obtained as the island lacks a formal information centre, and interpretative materials are only available in Vietnamese. While the Historical Museum does offer informal referrals, neither staff nor the displays provide information on the park or tourism-related facilities nearby, and the guides who lead tours of the prisons speak only Vietnamese.

At present, almost all of the money and operating equipment for CNDP comes from international donors, lending institutions or visitor fees, with very little contributed by the government of Vietnam itself. This dependence on foreign aid, while certainly necessary because of the lack of adequate funding from the national government, has impeded some innovative park efforts because staff feel hindered by the stipulations that accompany this assistance. The lack of adequate finances has also forced the park director to selectively manage certain natural and historical resources, while ignoring the conservation and protection of others.

Political challenges also exist. As many of Vietnam's current and recent leaders were incarcerated on Con Dao, the national government must formally approve all development related to CNDP (the current *1993–2010 Master Plan* was finalised at the Prime Minister Level, an event unique for a district level plan in Vietnam). In addition, consent from the military and Border Army is often required before entrance into certain areas is permitted, and visitors must surrender their passports when travelling between islands within the park.

Sustainable Tourism Initiatives

To respond effectively to the socio-economic, political, and environmental challenges it faces, a number of critical step have been undertaken by park officials since 1999. Some of the actions are institutional, while others are more personal in scope but equally constructive. Each effort, however incremental, is designed to foster greater co-operation between government agencies at the district and national level, and to broaden decision-makers' appreciation of the crucial role played by the park's ecosystem both ecologically and economically.

Among the more wide reaching measures undertaken are those by the Asian Development Bank (ADB), in collaboration with WWF-Indochina, to build more decision-making capacity at the local level, and to promote the sustainable use of coastal and marine resources in the western portion of the South China Sea (or 'East Sea' in Vietnam). An eco-tourism planner and a marine biologist hired by WWF assisted local staff in preparing an environmental and educational assessment of the park's biology and tourism resources in 1999–2000, and additional staff training in eco-tourism practices, interpretation, and guiding is planned or already under way. Meanwhile, capital investments are being solicited for conservation, interpretation, and the construction of eco-tourism-related facilities on Con Dao, Hon Bay Canh, and Hon Cau islands.

Aware that conservation also depends upon the cooperation and support of the local population, officials from the park and district government now support greater community awareness and use of its resources. On Con Dao, the Minister of Agriculture and Rural Development has plans to develop a small agricultural site within the park to provide fruits and vegetables for residents, and local school teachers are encouraged to participate in conservation activities that enable students to appreciate the park's biodiversity and the challenges facing protected areas in Southeast Asia. In Ho Chi Minh City, the Faculty of Tourism at Van Lang University has implemented an internship programme on the island for Vietnamese students and residents interested in acquiring practical experience in eco-tourism and natural resources management.

A second training programme jointly developed by CDNP and the Provincial Tourism Department, with the co-operation of the Border Army, is also now under way to licence local boat operators to ferry eco-tourists to islands for camping, wildlife viewing, swimming, and snorkelling. This will provide economic and educational benefits for local residents, and hopefully, encourage them to support conservation efforts in the park. The combined steps will also enable the director of CDNP and district officials to identify and manage the issues of highest priority.

To further minimise any unintended ecological impacts, the environmental management plan recently prepared for the park by WWF staff designated specific restricted-use zones to protect Con Dao's coral reefs, sea grasses and mangrove forests. These areas are the primary habitats for most of the 44 endangered plant and animal species listed in the *Vietnam Red Book* for CDNP. As part of that zoning activity, seven functional areas for managing the marine and terrestrial areas according to use have been proposed:

1. strict protection, scientific research, and limited eco-tourism;
2. turtle nesting beaches;
3. dugong/sea grasses;
4. rehabilitation of the natural environment;
5. marine eco-tourism areas;
6. limited natural marine resource development; and
7. port/harbour development.

A zoning group has already been formed to collect relevant scientific and biological information to determine the specific functions and site locations of the designated zones. Upon completion of the analysis and boundary maps, the park managers will propose specific regulations to govern permissible activities in each area according to their intended function: resource protection, scientific research, or eco-tourism and port development. Until such information has been obtained and approved, maximum daily limits on visits to sensitive sites have been established. These limits range from a high of 30 visitors (including 18 overnight campers) for Hon Cau, to a total of only six hikers (subject to district and military approval) on the trail to Nui Tanh Gia. These restrictions are intended to assure a quality experience for eco-tourists seeking to enjoy nature, while minimising disturbances to wildfire and marine life. They also reflect the park staff's limited ability to manage tourists and to simultaneously perform their conservation and enforcement duties.

Further Management Recommendations

To support the park's efforts to conserve biodiversity, and the district's efforts to develop alternative sources of income and employment for local residents, the following activities and guidelines are suggested for consideration in Con Dao's final management plan. The suggestions acknowledge the financial constraints that currently impede the park director's efforts to provide more meaningful interpretation of Con Dao's history and resources. They also take advantage of the human and environmental resources currently available, and the attention and assistance available through international organisations, such as the ADB and WWF.

Funding

As it is difficult to distinguish between visitors who come to Con Dao as eco-tourists and those who come for other purposes, all non-residents pay a single, multi-tiered entrance fee on arrival (students are exempt to encourage greater use of the park for educational purposes, while foreign residents pay more than Vietnamese nationals). Along with concession fees private operators within the park would be charged, and a proposed one-time Conservation Development Charge levied against all new construction on district land. All income would go into a Conservation Fund and the money then used only for environmental education and protection in the park or Con Dao district.

The Conservation Fund would be jointly administered by representatives of CDNP and the District, with earnings divided equally. This single fee would replace the separate admission fee charged by the Museum, as well as entrance fees to the national park. However, 'user fees' would continue to be charged for any activity within the park that requires a park ranger to provide a service beyond his/her normal duties (such as interpreting natural and cultural features, guiding along an unmarked train, or leading a group of snorkellers). Other recreational programmes offered by CNDP or private businesses may also require the payment of additional user fees, including boat trips to the outer islands, overnight accommodation, bicycle rental, snorkelling, and diving. All tourism-related revenue, including the visitor entrance fees, concession fees, and Conservation Development Charges, would be deposited into the Fund. This money would be used only for the construction, maintenance, and operation of facilities related to eco-tourism, biodiversity conservation, and environmental education. Permissible areas of expenditure might include:

- opening a park interpretation and environmental education centre;
- exhibits and operation of the museum;
- training of guides for CNDP and the historic district;
- purchase of environmentally-sensitive natural areas, which may be privately owned;
- preservation of historical buildings; and
- the design and preparation of educational activities and displays for local schools.

To address any concerns that tourists might have with the fee structure, information given to them on arrival would describe specific projects financed with visitor revenue so that they know they are directly contributing to the protection of Con Dao's natural and historic resources. This process also helps assure residents that the costs and benefits of tourism development are fairly distributed.

Interpretation and conservation

Mechanisms for educating visitors to Con Dao about its history and marine environment are currently lacking. Perhaps the most important requirement in this regard is a visitor interpretation, environmental education centre. Such a centre would contain informative multilingual displays of Con Dao's natural and historic resources as well as maps and other visitor information needs. As regards maps, these would act to highlight scenic, cultural, and recreational attractions, as well as major walking trails, lookouts, etc.

For visitors and residents interested in participating more directly in conservation efforts, opportunities to actively assist park rangers in protecting sea turtles and mangroves in the park are needed, as is a system of trails for hiking, bicycling, and wildlife viewing. The park and district could also act to co-sponsor the development of a Youth Conservation Group in the form of a local non-governmental organisation. The goals of such a group would include increasing environmental awareness amongst those of similar age, and to undertake specific conservation-related projects that would be of benefit to the park and the district. In addition, youth members could be enlisted to help post signs throughout the park, supplemented with self-guiding brochures in several foreign languages, identifying significant natural features and cultural artifacts.

Accommodation

At present, there are three hotels on Con Dao island; however, several traditional, Vietnamese bungalows are planned for the smaller islands of Hon Cau and Hon Bay Canh. Utilising renewable materials and authentic building practices wherever feasible, these accommodations will be simply constructed, elevated on stills to minimise land disturbance, and built to blend into the natural environment. Self-composting toilets will be a feature of these properties and hirers will be responsible for removing non-compostable rubbish when they leave.

Camping facilities on each island could be constructed and operated by private concessions selected by the park manager. Capital for materials and construction would be provided by the concessionaire, with all specifications being first approved by a park-designated architect. Although the bungalows will be privately-funded, ownership would remain with the park. In exchange for providing the capital to construct the bungalows, the concessionaires would be granted an exclusive, long-term lease (not to exceed 10 years) to use the buildings for eco-tourism-related purposes only. The concessionaires would also be entitled to 90 per cent of the gross revenue (10% of the gross revenue would be contributed to the Conservation Fund described elsewhere). Upon satisfactory completion of the initial lease period, concessionaires would be required to submit a competitive bid to renew their leases but may—at the discretion of the park director—receive preference in the selection process. To ensure that visitors do not negatively affect vegetation, water quality, or turtle nesting areas on each island, park rangers would supervise all construction and tourism activities.

Conclusion

The central task for residents, tourists, local governments, and the tourism industry on Con Dao is to develop and market a model of tourism that supports continuing visitation, while at the same time maintaining and enhancing the natural and cultural resource base upon which such visitation is based. Anxious to take advantage of the opportunities—and fully cognizant of the challenges—park managers and local residents of Con Dao have taken the first steps. While the recent nature of many of the actions outlined in the preceding sections prevent any firm conclusions being drawn, the initial impressions of staff directly involved in the planning and design process (including those from WWF, CDNP, the Forestry Planning Institute, and the Ba Ria-Vung Tau Provincial government) are that meaningful progress is being made towards the creation of a community-based tourism programme that is:

- sensitive to community concerns to maintain the cultural and natural heritage by limiting the number and character of visitors;
- inclusive, by mandating local participation in the planning and management process;

- capable of providing a mix of simple, efficient services to international visitors and Vietnamese residents alike; and
- ecologically and socially sustainable, incorporating both behavioural and biological parameters.

Indeed, so persuasive are the initial results and instructional support, the national government is now using Con Dao as the model for tourism development in the country's other national parks. Should Con Dao's experiment with alternative tourism prove successful over the long–term, it may also help stimulate similar projects in the Mekong and thereby create the basis for ongoing 'interdependent sub-regional growth and a firm foundation for sustainable development.'

9

Tale of Little Penguins and Tourists at Philip Island Nature Park

Much of Australia's natural heritage now lies inside national parks and reserves dotted island-like around the continent. Phillip Island Nature Park (PNIP) located near the entrance to Port Phillip Bay in the Australian state of Victoria is no exception. The park is surrounded by land long ago cleared for agricultural and pastoral pursuits as well as, in more recent times, for housing and recreational activities. This loss of habitat, combined with a range of other related factors, has seen the number of Penguin colonies on the island decrease dramatically to the point where today only one remains. The future of this colony, now protected within the PINP, has until relatively recent times also been in doubt. Tourism, it is argued in this case study, has been central in generating the resources and necessary political will to ensure the effective long-tern management of this last remaining colony.

This case study begins by overviewing the history of environmental management at, and visitation to, PINP. The significance of the economic benefits that flow to state and local economies from the Park's operations are then discussed, along with the role these have played in the site's preservation. The physical environment impacts that have resulted from visitation, along with other threats to the Park's environment, are then reviewed before examining the various approaches that have been employed to ameliorate these. The nature of current visitor experiences will then be addressed, before going on to examine how effective the present management regime has been in delivering these experiences in a sustainable way. Finally, selected issues regarding the role of tourism in the sustainable development of the Park will be discussed.

Background

Phillip island is located at the southern end of Western Port Bay, some 140 kilometres by road south of Melbourne. Europeans first settled Phillip island in the 1850 at which time there were ten Little Penguin colonies located along the island's shoreline. Clearing for agricultural and pastoral pursuits from the mid-1850s, and in more recent times, for housing and recreational purposes, was the primary causal agent in reducing this number to one by the beginning of the 1980s. Other factors identified as impacting upon penguin numbers include: the introduction to the island of predators (dogs, cats and foxes); the spread of exotic weeds that have acted to exclude penguins from their traditional breeding areas; and the introduction of rabbits with their similar habitat requirements, and whose feeding and burrowing activities caused significant erosion within traditional penguin breeding areas.

The last remaining penguin colony is located on a part of the island known as Summerland Peninsula, an area of approximately 340 hectares. This area had also been the subject of variety of land uses since human settlement, with the most significant, from the viewpoint of maintaining penguin numbers in the area, being a large housing subdivision. In 1927 a significant area of the peninsula was subdivided into residential blocks. This area was prime penguin habitat. Of the remaining land most was held by the local council: however, some in private hands, specifically the Spencer-Jackson family. This family began the process of reserving land for the use of Little Penguins when, in the early 1930s it donated four hectares to the local shire to be used as a penguin reserve. Shortly afterwards the Shire of Phillip island reserved additional land to which it later added in 1955. Partly fuelling the desire to protect the Little Penguin on the Summerland Peninsula was the nightly 'Penguin Parade,' which first began attracting visitors in the 1920s.

From the mid-1950s up until 1981 the local Shire controlled the reserve and managed the nightly 'Penguin Parade' which by the end of this period, had become a significant tourist attraction. In 1981, the Victorian state government, concerned by the way the site was being managed, and by statistics showing a significant decline in penguin numbers sought, control of the area through an amendment to the Crown Land Reserves Act. This amendment was passed and a committee to oversee the Park's management was established. The responsibilities of this committee were later expanded to include all other crown land and reserve on Phillip island. At this time the committee of management was reconstituted as the Philip Island Nature Park Board on Management (PINPBM). The goals of this new body were to:

- have the park recognised as a centre for excellence in wildlife conservation, research and education;
- conserve and enhance the wildlife and its habitat and other natural and cultural values of the park;
- provide opportunities for high quality ecotourism experiences and facilitate wildlife viewing and scenic viewing;
- provide outstanding and safe recreational opportunities for people with different needs and abilities;
- value staff and community input to park development and programmes;
- participate in regional, state and national tourism forums;
- train and develop staff to deliver high quality customer service and assist staff to reach their potential;
- maintain profitability and increase profit within the park in order to fund research, visitor facilities, conservation and management;

- provide leadership in co-operation with other bodies to access external funds for the economic development of the park, island and region; and
- ensure the park is managed as an efficient business.

With an eye to ensuring all key stakeholders are represented, the state government selects members of the PINPBM. The current committee totals twelve, with members being drawn from the following organisations and government departments:

- state government nominee (2);
- local tourism industry (1);
- local council (1);
- local community (2);
- Conservation Society (1);
- tertiary institution engaged in penguin research (1);
- tertiary institution engaged in koala research (1);
- financial adviser (1);
- friends of PINP (1); and
- park management (1).

A core responsibility of this board is the development and implementation of a management plan for the area. The most current of these was finalised in 2000 and involved taking into account some 173 submissions from the public and other interested organisations.

Economic Impact

It is doubtless, as Scrase notes, that the significant economic benefits at both a local and state level flowing from visitation to the 'Penguin Parade',[1] were instrumental in the decision by the Victorian Government to bring PINP under its control. The nightly 'Parade' of penguins returning to their burrows after a day's fishing at sea had become a significant component of Victoria's tourism product by the early 1980s. By 1993 Tourism Victoria estimated the annual net expenditure in the state arising directly and indirectly from the penguin parade at AU$50 million. A more recent estimate by the consulting firm KPMG has revised this figure upward to AU$96 million. Another study of economic impacts is due to be conduct in 2002.

Within the confines of Phillip Island itself, the Park had become the island's largest employer by the mid-1990s, with a total of 100 full-time and part-time staff, a figure that rises to 130 during the peak Christmas holiday season. The Park also injects over AU$2.2 million into the local economy in salaries as well as purchasing a significant percentage of its business inputs from island businesses or from nearby areas. It is also the case that many tourism and non-tourism businesses on the island benefit directly from tourist expenditure as a result of the stimulus provided by PINP.

In terms of direct income generated through PINP's own activities, admission fees raised approximately AU$4.6 million in 2000/2001, while other operating activities, essentially the sale of souvenirs and the provision of food and beverages, raised a further AU$3.5 million. In 2000/2001 these revenues resulted in an operating profit of approximately AU$1.1 million. This level of income has allowed PINP to be self-funding, with the exception of larger capital works programmes for which it must apply for government grants.

Visitation

While it is likely that some visitation to the area now encompassed by the Park took place prior to the late 1920s, it was not until that time that organised penguin viewing trips began to be run by some entrepreneurial island residents. These residents would meet visitors at the island's ferry and punt landings and escort them to Summerland Beach to watch the penguins arrive back at their nesting sites after feeding in the sea in the early evening. With the construction of a vehicular suspension bridge that linked the island to the mainland, visitation began to grow markedly. Over the next 40 years the popularity of the 'Penguin Parade' saw increasing numbers of intrastate and interstate visitors, as well as visitors from overseas, make the trip to Phillip Island. By the mid-1980s the 'Parade' attracted some 2,50,000. This number has since doubled, with visitors numbers reaching 5,20,000 in 2001, approximately 60 per cent of whom were from overseas.

A significant aspect of visitation to the Park is that it has now become highly industrialised from a tourism industry perspective, with 50 per cent or more of visitors arriving on packaged tours. This is particularly the case with overseas visitors where it is estimated more than 80 per cent purchase pre-packaged day tours to PINP.

Physical Environmental Impacts and Management Responses

From the time of the first organised tours to Phillip Island Nature Park (PINP) in the 1920s until the first efforts to control visitors access to the site in the mid-1960s, some degradation of the area's physical environment occurred. Specifically these impacts resulted from a desire by visitors to ensure a close 'first hand' experience of the penguin 'Parade.' To achieve this goal it was common for visitors to trample (and collapse) penguin burrows as they made their way to and from the beach, and to create their own track in doing so. This latter impact saw some destabilisation of dunes adjacent to the beach occur, reducing their value as a penguin habitat. It was also common for visitors to try to handle the penguins and to further stress them through the use of close range flash photography. Additional problems evident during this time were deaths resulting when penguins crossed the main access road and losses sustained from introduced predators, primarily foxes.

In the late 1960s it became evident to the local shire that the penguin colony under its care was to some extent in danger of being 'loved' to death.' The first step taken to ameliorate problems flowing from visitation was the construction of fences and viewing platforms with the intent of discouraging visitors from entering penguin nesting areas. Few additional efforts were made at managing visitation to the site through until the beginning of the 1980s. An incident in 1980 in which 136 penguin were killed deliberately by the driver of a motor vehicle, did result in all roads, other than the main access roads, being closed to visitors from dusk until dawn.

By the early 1980s researchers were concerned that a significant decrease in the number of breeding Little Penguins within the Park was occurring. Although it must be noted that visitation to the site was not seen as a major contributing factor to the declining penguin numbers. This situation was conveyed to the then state government, who, concerned for the welfare of the penguin and the maintenance of the significant economy that had built up around them, placed the Park under its control in 1981. As part of this process a new Committee of Management was formed that was required to:

> Protect the Little Penguin population and its environment, make them available for viewing by the public, generate a store of knowledge to educate the public and have the on-going means to attract visitors and funds to support management of the Park.
>
> **(Newman)**

Over the next 4 years the Committee of Management set about developing a Penguin Protection Plan (PPP). This plan was completed in July 1985, and involved the:

- allocation of funds for scientific research into the Little Penguin;
- purchase of a nearby housing development, Summerland Estate, and the staged rehabilitation of this land as penguin habitat; and
- development of a comprehensive site management plan.

It is particularly noteworthy in the context of this plan that the Victorian state government agreed to fund the purchase of an entire housing estate comprising 780 allotments, 180 of which contained houses, over a 15-year period. At the time of writing, this process is not yet complete; however, the government continues to honour its obligation, purchasing a further two houses and seventeen vacant allotments in 2000, by which time 84 per cent of the estate had been returned to public ownership. This is perhaps the first, and only, example in the Australian context of an instance where a (human) community has been essentially displaced for the good of a particular animal species. Arguably such action would not have been taken without the presence of the significant tourism economy that had built up around the Little Penguin.

The site management plant component of the PPP acknowledged the need to more effectively deal with rising levels of visitation. While noted previously, the effect of tourism on the Little Penguin colony had been slight, visitation was nonetheless rising, and the potential for a significant increase in visitor related impacts was therefore a very real one. To deal with this issue steps were taken to more effectively isolate visitors from penguins, while at the same time trying to ensure the maintenance of quality visitor experiences. To achieve these dual outcomes a substantial redevelopment of a section of the Park's beachfront area took place. This redevelopment, at a cost of some AU$3.6 million, was funded largely by the Park itself with some contribution from the Federal and state governments, and involved the construction of:

- beach viewing stands capable of seating approximately 4,000 people, which are designed for optimum viewing;
- elevated boardwalks that facilitate visitor access to the beach without disturbing the sensitive coastal dune systems—the penguins' home. These boardwalks also provide a viewing platform overlooking the penguin colony, and allow unrestricted access for penguins to their burrows; and
- a visitor centre, containing interpretative displays, printed material and audio-visual facilities.

Since these developments have occurred a further AU$3 million has been spent on improving on-site displays, enhancing commercial facilities (notably the restaurant and shop), expanding the sealed parking area and improving the lighting in this area, and building a penguin rehabilitation facility. This latter facility treated 346 penguins in 2000, the majority of these for oil contamination.

Financial resources generated by visitation have also been used to develop programmes and practices designed to: eradicate feral animals (sixty-nine foxes and sixty-eight cats were trapped/killed inside the Park in 2000); educate local community members to the responsible care of domestic pets; control introduced plant species; relocate penguins to rehabilitated areas; and replant degraded areas. As regards this last point, some tens of thousands of trees, shrubs and other native plants have been planted on the Summerland Estate in an effort to restore it to its pre-European state.

PINP's Board, it should be noted, is aided by volunteers in its efforts to manage the park environment and penguin colony. These individuals are involved in a variety of programmes including: providing interpretation services to visitors; weed eradication; rescuing wildlife and seed collection and propagation.

Research is also a core aspect of PINP activity, with its latest research strategy having been approved by its Board in February 2000. This strategy embraces such actions as: providing assistance to post-graduate students engaged in penguin research; seeking research grants; commissioning studies; and participating in collaborative research/activities with universities and other bodies (*e.g.*, in 1999 PINP joined with the International Union for the Conservation of Nature, and other interested organisations, in the preparation of a conservation and management plan for world penguins).

The Visitor Experience

Providing quality experiences for what can be up to 4,000 paying visitors on a single night is a major challenge. To achieve this goal access to the Park is only provided via the interpretative Centre where visitors can interact with a large range of displays detailing such matters as the life cycle of penguins, the dangers they face, and their habitat requirements. This Centre also contains a small theatrette, a cafeteria and a large shop where items ranging from toy penguins, film and items of clothing can be purchased. Additionally rangers are available to answer any questions.

Access to the beach is via raised boardwalks, along which a number of interpretive displays are located. In addition to these, signs stating that cameras are not be used to photograph penguins appear at regular intervals. Once at the beach visitors view from two large purpose built viewing stands. Alongside these stands is a series of lighting towers used to illuminate the beach area just after dark when the penguins arrive. Between the stands a tower has been constructed upon which sits a small commentary box. From this box a ranger provides information to visitors concerning the 'parade.'

In addition to the commentary, instructions are provided concerning such matters as the importance of staying on fenced paths. It is noteworthy that the continued non-observance of an instruction not to use flash photography by a small percentage of visitors ultimately led to the PINPBM banning cameras from being used altogether in October 1999. Instead, good quality and moderately priced photographs were made available for purchase in the Visitor Centre. Interestingly, Penguin Parade staff observed that this decision has had the effect of encouraging visitors to relax and enjoy the experience more. Rangers have also found that they are able to provide more information, and pay more attention to the needs of visitors, as they are not constantly having to remind them of the importance of not using flash photography.

In the period immediately leading up to the parade, and immediately after it, rangers are strategically positioned at the beach front, at viewing platforms, and along walkways, to act as both an interpretive resource and to ensure that visitors act in accordance with the guidelines provided to them. Once the parade is finished, visitors return via the Interpretive Centre where they can again access the various displays before leaving. Departing visitors are also asked to be careful when leaving the Park as approximately fifteen penguins a year are killed by cars.

As noted earlier, the majority of visitors are from overseas. In response to this, PINP has: employed a mandarin speaking ranger to liaise with tour groups; translated its Interpretive Centre audio visual programme into Mandarin and Japanese; and produced a taped commentary and visitor's guide in a number of languages. Pre-recorded instructions given at the parade itself regarding appropriate behaviour have also been prepared in several languages.

In addition to servicing the needs of parade visitors, a variety of education and interpretive services are provided to school and university groups. In 2001 PINP's rangers delivered education programmes to some 12,350 students. Additionally, a further 2,175 people participated in the activities programme which included snorkelling, presentations on penguins, and short interpretive walks dealing with seals and seabirds. Other information and interpretive services provided by PINP include a website (http://www.penguins.org.au), a newsletter (*Philip Island Nature Watch*), and a column in the local newspaper designed to inform the local community of wildlife activity in the park.

To assist the Board of Management in meeting the needs of visitors, marketing research is conducted on a regular basis (the latest being 2000) to determine basic demographics as well as the degree to which visitor expectations are being met. The outcomes of these surveys are used to refine service delivery systems. Additionally, when large changes to the site and its services are planned, research is conducted with visitors to gain their perspectives on these changes. For example, in 1995, prior to the redevelopment of the Interpretive Centre, an extensive survey was conducted to identify the type and level of information required by visitors as well as the on-site services (*e.g.*, food and beverage outlets and opportunities to purchase souvenirs) they required.

Assessing the Outcomes

The various management plans that have been implemented since 1985 have played a significant role in turning around a situation that, if allowed to continue, would have likely seen the penguin colony cease to exist by the mid-1990s. Penguin numbers have now returned to their estimated post-World War II numbers (28,000–30,000). Additionally, the production of chicks, as estimated from six study sites, is now 1.11 per breeding pair. This figure is well above the average for the past 30 years. Moreover, the Parle's plant life has been substantially restored with the result that erosion has been virtually eliminated and other species, particularly the Short-tailed Shearwater, now breed within the Park's perimeter. Significantly, from a tourism perspective, these results have been achieved in an environment that has seen visitor numbers grow by a factor of two over the 17-year period since 1985 when the first management plan was put into effect.

Other Issues and Concluding Comments

The processes employed at PINP, and their success in conserving the threatened Little Penguin colony, raise some important issues as regards tourism and natural resource conservation. Firstly, in the presence of significant economies based around visitation, those engaged conservation are likely to find their options constrained in the sense that there will be significant pressure to factor the maintenance and growth of visitation into their decision-making processes. Related to this point is the potential that such economies have to be used by individuals/organisations with a conservation agenda to 'push' governments and other stakeholders in that direction. In the case of PINP it is extremely questionable whether the state government would have acted to buy back an entire real estate subdivision on the basis of an argument built solely around the protection of the Little Penguin colony. Indeed, the Charter of the Board of Management established by the state government clearly reflects the significance of visitation and economic considerations in its operation.

Secondly, the PINP case demonstrates the capacity of highly structured 'experience' delivery systems underpinned by a 'hardened' environment, to meet the needs of visitors while at the same time minimising environmental impacts. This system has been extremely successful in controlling visitor movement on site; the time they spend on site; the type of interaction that takes place between them and the penguins; and their general behaviour. Indicative of this success, as Dann notes, is the similar rate of breeding in areas affected by tourism to those of adjacent areas without public access, and the absence of any penguin movement away from the tourist area. The 'gated' nature of such systems also means that visitation can generate a significant revenue stream that can be used for conservation purposes. In this regard almost AU$500,000 was spent on research, education and interpretation and Park protection in 1999/2000. The downside of such systems, however, has been the need to sacrifice some natural values in parts of the Park in order to construct the necessary infrastructure. In the case of PINP approximately 10 per cent of the penguin nesting area is open to public visitation, while an area of approximately four hectares is taken up by car parks and an interpretive Centre.

Thirdly, the capacity of humans to relate to a species, to see them as cute, 'touchable' or exotic, can be a significant factor in the conservation process. Without the 'bond' visitors to the Park feel with the Little Penguins, an industry would not have built up around them and arguably the forces acting for their conservation would have been far weaker. This observation is of relevance to natural area managers as it raises the issue of leveraging this bond not only to protect particular species but also other less 'appealing' animals that share the same habitat. In the case of PINP, the Board of Management has been able to use the income from the Little Penguin 'parade' to successfully manage the full range of species within the Park, including Short-tailed Shearwater, Western Water Rats, Little Forest Bats and Mutton-Bird. In the case of the Short-tailed Shearwater, funding for a programme designed to rescue and release birds that come into contact with power lines or other obstacles (a recurring problem with juvenile Shearwaters attempting their first migration) has been provided. This programme resulted in some 686 birds being rescued in 1999/2000.

Lastly, this case study displays how effective conservation can take place in the context of rising visitor levels, providing a holistic management strategy is adopted. The key ingredients of such a strategy, as demonstrated here, are: a primary focus on resource conservation; generation/provision of adequate financial resources to perform the conservation task; research; and a highly industrialised visitor experience delivery system built around an understanding of their needs.

10

Maho Bay Resorts: A Paradise

Developing appropriate tourism facilities and accommodations in fragile environments requires inspiration, innovation and technical ingenuity. Ecolodge developers contend both with the challenge of finding ways to build in harmony with nature and the need to engage visitors in nature-based experiences so that they have an enhanced understanding of the environment around them. This case study details how one ecolodge developer, Maho Bay Resorts (MBR) in the US Virgin Islands, has sought to address these challenges. In so doing MBR has sought to encompass the philosophy of sustainability in its broadest sense, extending beyond the environmental dimension to embrace economic and social goals linked to surrounding communities.

Maho Bay Resorts

Located on the island of St. John in the US Virgin Islands' National Park, Maho Bay Resort operates four properties: Maho Bay Campground, Harmony Studios, Estate Concordia Studios and Concordia Eco-Tents. Maho Bay Campground (MBC) opened in

1974 with 18 tent-cottages hidden among trees, and connected by elevated wooden walkways. The ecologically sensitive construction, land use and operations associated with the development stimulated significant media attention, which in turn generated strong growth in market demand. Since 1974, another 96 tent cottages have been constructed, resulting in the campground covering some fourteen acres. Harmony studies (HS), comprising 12 two-storey luxury units located on a 3-acre site on a hillside above Maho Bay Campground, was the next 'product' to be developed. Estate Concordia Studios (ECS), another luxury development comprising nine units, followed. The most recent 'product' to come on line is the Concordia Eco-Tents (CET), a more up-market version of the MBC tents. Both the CET and ECS developments are on a 5-acre site on the south-eastern shore of St. John Island.

As would be expected, significant differences exist between the construction costs of these different forms of resort accommodation. The original tent-cottages at the Maho Bay Resort campground can be constructed at a cost of about US$7000 each, while the luxury units at Harmony Resorts and Estate Concordia Studios cost in the vicinity of US$80,000. The Concordia Eco-Tent, developed after guest feedback indicated a preference for the same close-to-nature experience as offered by the MBC, but with private baths, running water and kitchen facilities, cost in the vicinity of US$ 30,000 per unit, including walkways and individual utility systems. These construction costs, even those of the more expensive HS and ECS resorts, are significantly less than those of the more traditional forms of tourism facility development found in the region.

Market demand for the various MBR products has been strong with occupancy levels approaching 100 per cent in the high season (mid-December to mid-April), while off-season occupancy rates are significantly above the norm for the Caribbean as a whole.

Sustainability Practices

The Maho Bay Resorts' Mission Statement reflects a commitment to sustainable tourism development:

> To provide a positive and educational experience for our guests while continuing to pioneer the principles of profitable, environmentally sensitive tourism (www.maho.org.).

This mission is reflected in MBR's efforts to: reduce environ-mental impacts flowing from its operations; conserve the islands' natural environment; educate guests regarding environmental matters; and engage with the local community.

Minimising Environmental Impact

The facilities at Maho Bay were built by hand and without large-scale clearing or road construction. First, boardwalks were constructed above the ground with manually dug holes for the posts. In this way disturbance to existing animal and plant communities was minimised. Over these boardwalks 'green' construction materials were then carried in. These materials included a range of recycled items such as old automobiles, bottles and garbage bags; composite timber for framing; and a range of energy efficient building products. The underside of these same boardwalks was later used to carry electrical and other services, thus avoiding the need to dig trenches. All site construction took place around existing vegetation, ensuring that the area remained as pristine and natural as possible, thereby eliminating the need for any extensive rehabilitation.

Steering MBR's operational philosophy are the three 'Rs' (reduce, reuse, recycle). A brief summary of the approaches in each of these areas follows.

Reduce

MBR seeks to reduce its use of resource inputs in a variety of ways, including:

- using spring-loaded taps to reduce water wastage;
- employing low-flush toilets, that save up to three gallons per flush over regular toilets, and waterless urinals;
- using water storage tanks on nearly all buildings in order to minimise dependence on energy-intensive and ecologically

damaging desalinated water, and to reduce energy costs associated with 'pumping' water;
- using unheated water in the bathrooms of most accommodation types;
- reducing guest energy usage by having all electrical devices (except the refrigerator in units that are so equipped) automatically turn off when a guest locks their doors behind them;
- serving draft soda and beer instead of bottled beverages;
- ordering restaurant and retail store supplies that require minimal packaging;
- purchasing bulk kitchen and housekeeping supplies;
- employing 100 per cent biodegradable laundry detergent and limiting the amount of bleach used to a minimum, allowing resultant wastewater to become a viable water source for secondary usage; and
- using photovoltaics as the main power source for the resort (MBR is not connected to the island's electricity grid), and additionally employing in the Concordia Eco-Tents, wind generators and passive solar water heaters.

Reuse

Examples of MBR's reuse practices include:

- the 2,000–7,000 gallons of nutrient rich effluent water generated by MBR's wastewater treatment plant each day is used to water an organic orchard that provides food for the resort;
- all houseware items supplied in the tent-cottages and restaurant are reusable;
- packing and shipping boxes are returned to suppliers, who refill them with the resort's next order; and
- a 'Help Yourself Centre' allows guests to leave items they no longer require so that these products can be used by other visitors.

Recycle

A range of innovative actions are in evidence as regards recycling practices, including:

- composting food, paper and cardboard waste to nourish an organic garden and orchard;
- melting down aluminium on site and using it to create functional and decorative items for sale through the resort's shop;
- using the residue from composting toilets in the planting of indigenous trees and shrubs; and
- crushing glass to use as aggregate in cement, or to recycle into new glassware using the resort's kiln.

In addition to practising the three 'Rs' MBR has a policy of purchasing recycled products wherever possible. Many of the items used in the construction of the resort were composed of recycled, or largely recycled, material. For example, the wood used in construction of the walkways and railings of the Harmony suites is a wood polymer composite lumber, made from recycled plastic and sawdust. Additionally, all nails used were made from recycled steel, as were some furnishings (*e.g.*, recycle rubber tyre rugs, and the tiles used for counter and table-tops).

Conservation of Natural Resources

Associated with MBR's concern regarding minimising its environmental impacts is its commitment to ensuring the long-term protection and conservation of the natural resource base on which its future depends. In this regard, it has sought to maintain and enhance the natural environment in and around its developments by using a variety of means. These include: employing only indigenous vegetation in the landscaping process; establishing unobtrusive sites from which visitors can view the island's wildlife (*e.g.*, birds, mongooses lizards and other animals); and educating guests regarding the need to refrain from feeding animals so that they may remain wild and independent from human influence. The elevated walkways MBR has constructed also reflect the extent to which it has gone to maintain the quality of its environment. There are three miles of these wooden walkways, laid out in such a way that they avoid site features such as trees and rocks, or accommodate them (as is the case with some trees) by cutting a hole through walkway timbers. The elevated nature of these structures also allows for the free movement of animals around the site. Other, less direct means of conserving the natural environment employed by MBR include a policy that prohibits the purchase of products known to originate from endangered plants or animals.

Education

The very structure and design of MBR's facilities provides its guests with numerous opportunities to learn about such matters as alternative energy use, waste reduction and resource conservation methods. Indeed, in 1998 Stanley Selengut, the owner of MBR, made this point clear when he noted that 'there's a secondary purpose to these dwellings. It's not just to have them work well, it's also to have them function as a teaching machine.' Perhaps the most obvious example of this is the computer system that has been installed in the Harmony Resort units that allows guests to monitor their own energy and water consumption, thereby helping them to understand the relationship between their consumption patterns and available resources.

MBR also seek to encourage its guests to learn and interact with the island's physical environment. With this goal in mind, an interpretive trail has been constructed through the resort area that provides insights into local plants and wildlife. In addition, nightly presentations on the ecological and cultural history of the area are provided to give the guests a greater appreciation of the resort's ecological context. Resort staff are also encouraged to explain to guests aspects of the resort's design and operations that are acting to reduce impacts or generally enhance the environment. This kind of dialogue and interaction can serve to transform a holiday into a memorable learning experience. As a further means of fuelling guest interest in environmental matters, MBR has decided to encourage its guests to become members of the International Ecotourism Society (IES) during the United Nations International Year of Ecotourism in 2002. Such encouragement takes the form of deducting the price of membership for IES, a part of the worldwide movement towards less environmentally damaging tourism, from the cost of a stay at any of its properties.

In a broader context, MBR's design and operational practices can be said to have provided a model for low impact sustainable tourism ventures. In 1991; for example, the United States National Park Service conducted a workshop on sustainable design at Maho Bay Campground. Attendees included participants from the American Institute of Architects; American Society of Landscape Architects; the Ecotourism Society; National Parks and Conservation Association; National Oceanic and Atmospheric Administration; Green-peace; local representatives from the Virgin Islands; private architectural and engineering firms; and ecotourism resort operators. As a result of this workshop the National Park Service and MBR formed a partnership to produce the first prototype design guidelines for sustainable campground design (see Appendix). In 1994, MBR was also the host of the First International Ecolodge Development Forum and Field Seminar. At this meeting scientists and practitioners were provided with a rare opportunity to share creative ideas and methods for operating economically viable and ecologically sensitive ecolodges, while at the same time experiencing an example of such. Following on from its involvement in such events, MBR will in 2002 host a five-day workshop on photovoltaic technology run by Solar Energy International. MBR is also the subject of a video by Clean Islands International Inc. that is shown to school students and various other groups in the Caribbean region.

Community Involvement

While initially focusing on dimensions of sustainability, MBR has more recently sought to stress the development of more socially and culturally sustainable practices. Evidence for this can be found in: the employment of local residents whenever possible; the purchasing of most services and supplies from local sources; and the engagement of local artists to entertain guests. Additionally, MBR strives to work in a spirit of mutual co-operation with its local community.

An innovative means by which MBR is seeking to contribute to the cultural life of St. John Island is its Recycled Art Centre. This centre seeks to explore any and all forms of art that can be made out of recycled materials (*e.g.*, pottery, mosaics, painting, photography, paper-making, fibre art, glass blowing, jewellery, bead-making, woodworking and metal work) and invites interested artists to visit, dividing their time on an equal basis between working at the resort and being artist in residence at the centre.

Conclusion

Maho Bay Resorts has been, and remains, very much a pioneer in the creation and development of sustainable resort development practices. At MBR these practices are reflected in its commitment to protecting the physical environment and in its efforts to ensure the resort provides benefits to the community in which it is located. MBR has demonstrated that it is indeed possible to provide for the comfort and enjoyment of guests, preserve the natural resource base on which the future delivery of such benefits are based, and operate a sustainable business. The extent of MBR's success is evident in its use as an 'experimental' model by the US National Parks Service, and its hosting of various events concerning ecolodge design and operations. The guiding approach to MBR's efforts to date is perhaps best summed up by its owner, Stanley Selengut, who noted: 'I am not a philosopher, but if I have learned anything about sustainable design over the past twenty years, it is that it is ego-less. It is about what works and listening to bath nature and your customers.'

Appendix

Design guidelines for the Maho Bay/National Park Service Agreement to Develop Prototype Sustainable Campgrounds

This document and the prototype guidelines were developed to provide prospective architects with design specifications for our future projects. It addresses three main topics: the Structure and Design of Prototype Eco-tent Dwellings; Eco-tent Conservation; and Additional Site Uses. Each section covers specific structural elements that should be included in sustainable design, as well as examples from the Maho Bay eco-tents and suggestions for education and interpretation in units.

Prototype eco-tent dwelling—structure and design

Sustainable design balances human needs (rather than human wants) with the carrying capacity of the natural and cultural environments. It minimises environmental impacts, importation of goods and energy, as well as generation of waste. The ideal situation would be that if development was necessary, it would be constructed from natural sustainable materials collected on site, generate its own energy from renewable sources such as solar or wind, and manage its own waste.

Eco-tent designs must be:

Affordable—building costs should be under US$30,000 per unit, including walkways and individual utility systems.

Vernacular and site specific—incorporating the natural landscape as well as some local character.

Location

- Place the site-adaptive eco-tents on the more pristine and fragile setting of the site.
- Build solid support building on the worst, or previously damaged sections.
- Avoid visual pollution of the landscape.

Background: At Maho, sensitive siting combined with ecological restoration has actually repaired some of the local environment. If it is necessary to build a swimming pool, it should be located on sloping terrain to accommodate the slope of the bottom of the pool, perimeter footings can be hand dug, if necessary. Tennis courts, etc., should be built on flat terrain, etc.

Size

- The units should be as small as possible to fit within existing trees and topography.

  Background: Two optimum unit dimensions have worked well at Maho:

  Choice A = 16' × 16' footprint with a 2' × 8' extension for the open porch (the toilet and shower are outside the unit connected by the walkway).
  Choice B = 16' × 16' footprint with a porch area outside the unit connected by the walkway (in this version the toilet and shower are inside the units).

Interior design

- The units should sleep a family of four with privacy and comfort, and up to six people, if necessary.

Background: A 16' × 16' square floor plan can be divided into four 8' × 8' sections: a bedroom, kitchen area, living room with a queen-size sleep sofa, and either an open porch or a toilet shower area. The bedroom should be a bit larger to accommodate two twin beds with some space in between, a sleeping loft can hold an additional two children. Extending the porch 2' would allow for a larger bedroom.

Materials

The complete life-cycle energy, environmental, and waste implications of each building material must be examined. This cradle-to-grave analysis is the tracing of a material or product, and its by-products, from its initial source availability and extraction through refinement, fabrication, treatment and additives, transportation, use, and eventual reuse or disposal. This tracing includes the tabulation of energy consumed and the environmental impacts of each action and material.

- Units should use recycled and local building materials where possible.
- Materials should be light and portable.
- Structural members should have minimum standard dimensions.
- Materials should be used so that there is very little waste, for example if fabric is 64" and only 54" is needed, the additional material used for another purpose.

Background: Maho has been successful with a light wood framed structure, supported on 4"+4" posts and covered with heat reflective fabric for the roof and nylon-reinforced, laminated fabric for the walls. Other ideas might be considered for different climates or situations, for example metal framing instead of wood, straw bale, rammed earth, or hemp for walls, etc.

Walkways

- The units should be connected by elevated walkways to minimise site disturbance.
- The walkways should allow easy access to difficult terrain at the campground.
- The walkways should be built first so that workmen and building materials can traverse the walk during construction.
- Electrical wiring and water pipes should be fastened to the underside of the decking.

Background: using an elevated walkway system are has allowed the Maho Bay resorts a minimum of site erosion over their twenty year history, even on a steep sloping site.

Construction

- The site is to be left as undisturbed as possible.
- Prefabrication should take preference to site building.

- The dwellings should be easy to build by low skilled labour, and sit on hand-dug footing or anchored to builders.
- Heavy construction equipment should be avoided.

The construction process is an integral part of the building plans. Where conflict exists, the decision should always be for the environment.

Background: Maho Bay uses only specialised heavy equipment which can work from roads to avoid site disturbance (*e.g.*, concrete pumps, back hoe, 4-in-1 bucket on our bulldozer, etc.)

Orientation

Units should be elevated to accommodate space for composting toilets and cisterns underneath the platform. Consideration should also be given to wind directions and sun angles:

- Units must support passive solar heating/cooling and energy production.
- Composting toilets should be located down wind.

Background: The tent, at Maho Bay are built on sloping terrain to provide room under the platform for the toilet and cistern. On flat land the platform should be elevated to a height over the compost bin.

Roof

- Roof should be designed to catch rainwater with drainage to a cistern.
- Roof should be heat reflective with overhangs to protect dwellings from intense mid-day sun

Background: Reflective coating and overhangs help to prevent heat from penetrating the dwelling, this is integral for passive cooling techniques. Water collected from the roof is filtered to be potable.

Storage space

- The tents should have plenty of pegs for hanging guest's clothes, as well as shelves/storage for luggage. It is important to use every inch of space.

Background: Storage space within the unit has been an issue in the Maho eco-tents.

Climate

- Units should be designed to protect the guests from changes in climate (wind, rain, temperature, etc.).

Background: The Maho Bay tents use screening, roll down shades, pulleys, bungee cords, etc., to allow for opening and closing the dwelling as necessary.

Natural disasters

- The units must deal with natural trauma (hurricane, rock slide, fire, earthquake, etc).

Background: In the Virgin Islands the major problems are termites and hurricanes. We use termite-proof building materials and furnishings which are weather resistant. We also use outdoor furniture, waterproof couch and bed coverings, stainless steel and marine fittings, Monel staples, etc. Fabric is connected to the structure by Monel staples so that the fabric blows loose in a hurricane and there remains little wind resistance on the structure. Screens are removable so they can be taken down before the hurricane. Tarp and ropes can be stored under units to cover the furnishings.

For California—consider solutions for fires, earthquakes, and rock slides (*e.g.*, controlled burning, etc.).

Atmosphere

- The units should provide a sense of privacy while maximising views and interesting natural 'assets'.
- The structures, however, should be subordinate to the ecosystem.

Background: Adequate space and vegetation between the units, and careful and creative sitting in the field can provide a sense of privacy and interest within the campground. Positive sensory experience are also important for the guest: sight, sound, touch, smell.

Landscape

- The campground should heighten the sense of intimacy that the guest has with the surrounding natural environment.

Background: Choose sites in interesting areas with a good view. The dwelling should be light, open, and toward views. Planting of aromatic and colourful native trees and plants will attract wildlife like hummingbirds. Planting is also used for privacy screening. This flora is supported by the compost from the toilet and grey water from the shower.

Restoration

- Sustainable site design requires holistic, ecologically based strategies to create projects that do not alter or impair but instead help repair and restore existing site systems.
- Development should address ecological restoration of the site.

Background: At Maho Bay it is necessary to control feral animals and exotic imported plants and trees. Initiation of a native plant landscaping programme has helped to attract indigenous wildlife. In the Virgin Islands the birds, bats, lizards, and tree frogs in turn help control the biting insects.

Eco-tent conservation

Energy: Responsible energy use is fundamental to sustainable development and a sustainable future. Energy management must balance the justifiable demand with the appropriate supply. The process couples energy awareness, conservation, and efficiency with the use of primary renewable energy resources. To sustain its own wise use of energy, the sustainable development must demonstrate benefits rather than sacrifices to its users (which includes visitors and operators).

Renewable electric power

- The units should be energy self-sufficient using renewable electric power and maximising passive solar design.

Background: The eco-tents at Maho Bay successfully use photovoltaics .and wind for electric power. Hydro and big-gas for energy might be appropriate in some cases.

Education: This is an interesting educational opportunity for the customer. When the batteries are full the guest is actually wasting by not using energy. It is important to encourage consumption when power is available and conservation when it is not.

- A gauge is necessary to monitor available energy in the battery, and indicate when batteries are full.
- A voltmeter allows guests to adjust solar panels to the optimum angle to the sun.
- A barometer helps with weather forecasting.
- An occupancy sensor should be used to minimise energy use when unit is not occupied.
- Timers on appliances to avoid overuse.

Ventilation and cooling

- Passive and natural techniques should be used.

Background: At Maho, the tents use solar design such as roof overhangs, heat reflective glass and fabric, and planting for shade, in conjunction with wind scoop ventilation, Venturi principle, and evaporative cooling. Other alternatives might be thermal chimneys, earth sheltering, etc.

Education: The best strategy for keeping a dwelling cool is to keep it from getting hot in the first place. That means shading to block the hot mid-day sun but not the cooling breezes. Cooling techniques can be more elusive than other aspects of the eco-tents, so it is important to post signs about:

- Evaporative cooling principles. .
- Ventilation by wind scoops and Venturi principle.
- Heat reflection by reflective fabric and glass.
- Shading—use of planting and trees, awnings and roof overhangs to protect from the sun.

Heating

- Guests should be able to sécure units to hold heat, as well as to open up units to maximise ventilation for cooling.

Background: There is no need for heating on St. John, although the eco-tents can be closed to trap in heat on cool nights. In colder climates the units should maximise solar design: mass for insulation, techniques such as circulated air heated by hot water storage inside the unit, or a back-up propane heater.

Education: Heating should be customer interactive; for example, a simple way to keep people warm is to layer more clothing.

Water supply and collection

- Units should have cistern-holding capacity which stores rain water collected from the roof.

Background: Since there is not always enough rain to accommodate guests, the cistern provides storage for rain water as well as water that is trucked in. Rain is collected off the roof and stored in a cistern (cisterns can be interconnected with overflows for alternate filling). The guest hand pumps water from the cistern into a black container over the shower which provides water pressure and functions as a hot water heater. This container feeds both the shower and sink and has gauges showing water level and temperature. If the water is too hot, the guest can pump more cold water from the cistern into the black solar heater. The gauge at the sink and the shower shows water use versus supply in the cistern, and total water use during the guest's stay (use low flow fixtures).

Education: User education and awareness is vital to a successful water conservation programme. Positive reinforcement should be provided to visitors by informing them of their actual water savings as well as their responsibility in achieving the goal of water conservation.

Fixtures

- The units should use energy efficient fixtures compatible with solar design.

Background: The Maho Bay camps use Sun Frost refrigerators, DC fans, microwave ovens, solar efficient lighting, compact fluorescent bulbs, solar pumps, a two burner stove run by propane, etc. Natural daylight should be used wherever possible.

For Hawaii—beach frontlighting should be designed not to disorient turtle hatchlings.

Lighting should be low intensity and directed downward or reflected with cut off angles, or set back from the beach so not directly visible.

Education: Use meters to show electric consumption by appliances. Timers on fans; appliances, and lights help to make guests aware of their energy use.

Waste

The only way to avoid environmental harm from waste is to prevent its generation. Pollution prevention means changing the way activities are conducted and eliminating the source of the problem. This does not mean doing without, but doing differently.

Composting toilets

- Human waste should be treated with a composting toilet.

Background: Several models of composting toilets have been experimented with at Maho Bay—a toilet with minimum water flush seems to work the best.

Education: The toilet must be designed with gauges showing heat and moisture content so the guest can monitor the health of bacteria in the compost. If the temperature drops in the bin, the guest adds organic material (*i.e.*, sawdust or food scraps) to the mass and stirs with a lever. If the compost pile gets too dry, the guest pumps water from the bottom over the mass. A sign placed near the toilet can provide interpretive information that explains to the guest how a composting toilet works.

Compost from toilets should be used for local planting.

Food waste

- Appropriate food waste should be disposed of in a composting bin, and the balance used for animal feed.

Education: The campground should be designed to promote food waste composting: provide an area for collecting scraps and install a programme for sensible use of compost.

Waste water

- Water conservation includes using water of lower quality such as reclaimed wastewater effluent, grey water, or runoff from ground surfaces, for irrigation of vegetative landscape or food crops.
- Where applicable, separate grey water (showers, sinks, etc.) from black water (toilet waste).
- Grey water should be filtered through a one-foot-wide stone through filled with soil and then used for drip irrigation.

Background: At Maho Bay, grey water is used to support vegetative growth, and rejuvenate indigenous plant and animal life in the area (natural drainage patterns should be taken into consideration). Nutrient rich grey water can be used to grow small gardens near or around units and also for producing food.

Back-up systems

- Units should have back-up support systems in case guests run out of power or water.

Background: At Maho Bay, there is propane back-up for cooking, candles for light, and public watering stations when necessary. The units are also equipped with a five gallon water container and an ice chest (ice is available at the commissary).

Additional site uses

Restaurant and eating pavilion
Performing arts pavilion
Dormitory housing for students

Teaching (classroom) facilities
Separate pavilion for conference/workshops, etc.
Swimming pool
Tennis courts
Other sports activities
Maintenance facilities (workshop/storage)
Food storage (freezer, refrigerator)
Commissary
Office space

Food production area

Located adjacent to the restaurant, possibly using a fish pond, planting shed, orchard, etc., to use wastewater and compost from the resort. The food will then be featured in the restaurant.

Workshop

Repairs, woodworking crafts, prototype development and product testing

Nature centre

Trail development, bird watching, plant identification, and wildlife sanctuary.

Research development and testing centre (outside funding needed)

- Development of sustainable electric power sources.
- Development of natural waste treatment systems.
- Development of smallscale manufacturing processes to convert local trash into building materials.
- Development of a solar kiln backed by propane to support local manufacturing of trash into building products.

11

The Fairmont Chateau Whistler Resort

This case study of the Fairmont Chateau Whistler Resort (FCW) illustrates how a hotel resort is actively contributing to sustainable tourism development by striving to operate within an environmentally, socially and economically responsible framework. The case sets the FCW apart from many other resort hotels for several reasons. It illustrates how a sustainability programme can be developed from a foundation of spontaneous environmental initiatives. Specifically, it describes how the FCW has developed a strategic programme from sustainability principles, outlines how this agenda has been implemented, and highlights some of the key environmental and social practices that have been undertaken.

However, before moving to discuss these matters, some background is provided on FCW itself and its parent company, Fairmont Hotels and Resorts.

Fairmont Hotels and Resorts

The FCW is part of Fairmont Hotels and Resorts, a Canadian company that manages national and international luxury hotels. Over the past decade this company has become a North American tourism industry leader and catalyst in 'greening' hotel operations. In 1990 the company's corporate office surveyed all employees to find out whether or not they would be supportive of an environmental programme. The survey determined that 91 per cent of employees strongly supported more environmentally responsible practices within the hotels where they worked. In response, a corporate greening programme called 'the Green Partnership' was launched across the company's hotel chain. Over the years, this programme has evolved from an environmental guidebook to a more comprehensive incentive and monitoring programme that is administered by a corporate environmental office. From the inception of the Green partnership programme, the FCW has actively participated in a range of environmental management pursuits.

Fairmont Chateau Whistler Resort

The FCW is an all-season hotel resort that opened in 1989. This chateau-style hotel is located in Whistler, British Columbia, approximately 120 km north of Vancouver. Whistler is a community that has evolved from the site of a few remote fishing lodges in the early 1960s into a world-class destination. The FCW resort is situated at the base of Blackcomb and Whistler mountains, overlooking the core of the village. FCW has 560 hotel rooms and employs over 600 staff. Its guest rooms are complemented with administrative space, six independent meeting rooms, three major ballrooms, a number of hospitality suites and a rooftop garden terrace. FCW's facilities also include two restaurants, a bar, a health club, spa, staff housing and an 18-hole golf course.

The Whistler area's beautiful mountain environment attracts not only visitors, but is also home to some 9,500 year-round residents. Largescale residential and commercial developments over the past two decades have placed extensive pressure on the natural ecology of the area, as well as on the social fabric of the community. The FCW recognises these stressors, and has made it a priority to minimise the negative impacts of its operations by undertaking programmes to enhance both the community and the area's natural environment.

The Sustainability Journey

As part of its involvement with its parent companies 'Green Partnership Programme,' FCW established a Green Team with representative from all hotel departments. This group was responsible for implementing many of the environmental initiatives suggested by the corporate programme. The success of this group's efforts have twice been acknowledged over the past ten years with FCW being awarded the title of 'Fairmont Environmental Property of the Year.' In addition, such efforts have seen FCW establish itself as a leader in environmental management in the Whistler community.

Building on its previous environmental management successes, in 2000 FCW embarked on a more ambitious set of initiatives. The first of these initiatives was the development of a vision of social responsibility for its staff, guests, the community, environment and other constituents. To enact this vision David Roberts, the General Manager of the FCW, who has a special appreciation of the natural beauty of Whistler, recognised that sustainability initiatives in the operations of FCW had to be taken to a more strategic level. While FCW was seeking answers as to how this might be done, the founder of The Natural Step (TNS) framework for sustainability was visiting Whistler and held several compelling presentations on this particular subject. As a result of these presentations FCW decided to join with five other organisations including private businesses, local government and a resident environmental group to collectively use TNS to create a shared vision for sustainable practices, not only for their own individual organisations, but for the entire Whistler community.

While FCW had long been dedicated to both environmental and social practices, there was no overall strategy that acted to guide and prioritise actions in these areas. Using TNS as its base, FCW began for the first time in 2001 to work towards the achievement of its vision of social responsibility in a strategic way.

Developing a Sustainability Programme

Systems

A successful sustainability programme requires awareness, understanding and commitment to sustainability goals from management and staff. In order to engage the leadership team, all FCW managers participated in a Whistler Sustainability Symposium that was organised by the local TNS group. To train staff, a group of in-house trainers underwent a 2-day TNS 'train-the-trainer' session. These individuals developed a sustainability awareness programme and delivered training for each department. To create a common language and awareness throughout the entire hotel operation, TNS training was also integrated into new employees' orientation programmes.

The FCW Sustainability Programme began with a preliminary environmental review to gain a better understanding of current resource flows and practices. From this review, four priority areas for improvement were chosen as an immediate focus for action. These were waste management, energy management, developing sustainable products and services, and community philanthropy. In addition, supply chain management was identified as an important strategic means for reducing environmental impacts.

Within FCW, Solution Teams were formed to identify and prioritise problems and actions in each of these areas. Team members were those individuals in the hotel resort who had the knowledge and position to implement change, such as the chief engineer, as well as other enthusiastic staff. To ensure resources and accountability, each of the Solution Teams was led by a member of the resort hotel's executive management group. Once the teams were formed, they participated in 'Ideas to Action' workshops, where they reviewed the current reality of FCW operations and envisioned an ideal, sustainable future for the hotel resort's operations. Based on the difference between this vision and the current reality, each team set its own measurable objectives for 2001. Projects to reach these objectives were then brainstormed, prioritised and selected. These projects continue to gain momentum and have been successful for several reasons. Firstly, member commitment was established because the teams defined their own objectives. Secondly, project goals were grounded in reality because the members were the experts within their own areas of operation. The members of the teams were also from different departments, so they learned to consider the challenges across all divisions rather then just in their own.

In order to monitor progress and demonstrate economic, environmental and social benefits, efforts are made to make team objectives measurable, and are designed to be tracked regularly. For example, the Waste Solution Team identified a 12 per cent reduction in waste to landfill as one of their objectives for 2001. In order to assure reliable measurements, the FCW installed a compactor where waste is accurately measured with each tipping. This is a change from previous volume-based weight estimates. Twenty-four hour waste audits have also been organised to biannually determine the composition of waste and to identify areas for improvement.

The teams review their progress on an ongoing basis, and the measurements are communicated to the rest of the Green Team members. Since the success of many of these initiatives depends directly on the participation of all employees, it is important that staff be constantly updated on progress. The executive management team reviews the process and outcomes of the programme annually at strategic retreat sessions.

Practices

Practices that contribute to environmental sustainability can also provide significant short- and long-term business benefits. Potential business benefits include cost savings, innovation, avoidance of future liability, improved staff morale and motivation, enhanced public reputation, increased market share and strengthened stakeholders' relationships. This section highlights FCW practices that have been successful in realising both ecological and business benefits.

Communicating and training

Management and staff understanding is central to the success of

FCW's environmental programmes. Staff need to understand the reasons for, and goals of, each programme in order to actively contribute. Programme leaders at the FCW understand this and facilitate the sharing of information in various ways. For example, the FCW has an internal Communications Committee that includes at least one representative from each department. The committee's monthly meeting is one means for receiving feedback to and from individual departments regarding environmental initiatives. Another highly effective means of communication is a mandatory weekly operations meeting among all managers. At these meetings sustainability activities are discussed on a regular basis. The FCW also has environmental bulletin boards in all departments and publishers a bi-weekly staff newsletter, called *Tell Me a Story*. This well-read newsletter contains an environmental column called *On the Green Front*. Another effective way in which FCW communicates environmental information is through 'green' theme days in the staff cafeteria. These are held at least three times per year.

Staff capacity with respect to participating in sustainable practices is also developed in many other ways. For example, each employee participates in TNS Awareness Training, and has a half-day of specific waste, energy and safety training as part of their official employee orientation programme. Other seasonal and departmental training activities supplement this programme. These include 'Black Bear Awareness Training' that is delivered every spring. FCW also has an ever-expanding library of literature dealing with sustainability issues, where interested staff can sign out books, videos and a newspaper scrapbook.

Staff training, however, is not simply about acquiring skills in order to undertake an immediate task at hand. It is also about building capacity and skills that enable employees to respond to changing demands and opportunities for new activities. Through the ongoing environmental education that the Chateau Whistler provides, employees are introduced to key elements of environmental responsibility as well as to techniques for implementing these stewardship ideals.

Reaching out and building awareness and capacity among external groups, such as guests, the community and business partners, is also very important. The FCW undertakes a growing number of initiatives in this regard. For example, both the hotel and the golf course are proactive in offering tours of their facilities to guests, schools and other interested groups. Over the past year, the FCW has hosted six groups from elementary school to university, who are interested in tourism and sustainable development practices. FCW representatives have also spoken at conferences and actively participated in community and social responsibility events, such as Clean Air Day and the British Columbia Ethics in Action Award programme. The hotel resort also sponsors educational talks and events by local individuals. These include a popular monthly slide-show series by a local bear researcher. Recognising the value of dialogue and group commitment, the FCW also hosted a community sustainability symposium as well as a corporate environmental conference in 2000.

Another method of communication with guests and residents is through interpretative signs at the golf course. These signs along the course's walking trails identify features such as native plants and their traditional uses, bird species frequenting the area, interesting historical occurrences, and information about local stream and fish ecology. Both residents and tourists appreciate this unique opportunity to learn and experience the natural environment and wildlife of the area.

Reducing, reusing and recycling

The FCW works to increase the efficiency of its resource use by reducing, reusing and recycling. Examples of resourceful ways of decreasing the resort hotel's material flows include: administration's decreased use of paper via extensive use of computer communication technology; the landscapers' efforts to hand-pull weeds rather than use toxic herbicides; the development of an organic herb garden on the roof-top patio in order not only to reduce reliance on pesticide, but also increase the property's ambience for guests. Different hotel departments are also using alternative products that are more environmentally benign. For example, the hotel kitchen is currently testing a new product to keep banquet food dishes warm. This product is made of renewable sugar cane, contains no toxic materials and is purchased in a recyclable container.

The hotel resort views all waste as an inherent inefficiency and is creative in reusing products wherever possible. For example, empty plastic pails from the kitchen are used by other hotel departments for maintenance purposes, or are taken by staff for personal use. Paper is recycled and bound into notepads or used for draft photocopying. Unused guest room amenities, such as soaps and shampoos, as well as larger items like furniture, are all donated to local charities. Some waste output has also been used as an input to make a completely new product. For instance, FCW has developed a partnership with a progressive regional company called international Bio-Recovery that makes high quality fertiliser out of food and organic waste. FCW provides the company with organic waste that is normally difficult to dispose of locally due to its attractiveness to the area's bears. The relationship with international Bio-Recovery serves to assist a local company, while diverting approximately 500 kilograms of waste from the community's local landfill on a daily basis.

If waste cannot be used, it is recycled whenever possible. The FCW has developed a comprehensive recycling programme in which efforts are made to ensure that as much sorting as possible occurs at the source. To make this process easier for employees, recycling stations are labelled and colour co-ordinated throughout the hotel resort. Even guests are engaged in the recycling efforts. FCW programmes demonstrate that many recycling initiatives can be implemented while meeting high guest standards. For example, recycling in guest rooms is encouraged with attractive wicker baskets that have four labelled compartments for different recyclable materials. These were custom designed and are found in every FCW guest room. Since the implementation of this programme, housekeeping waste going to landfill has dropped by over 30 per cent—from over 2 lbs (1 kg.) to 1.4 lbs (0.6 kg.) per guest per day. Guest rooms also have toilet paper, tissues and stationery, which are made from recycled materials.

Working with the supply chain

While reducing, reusing and recycling activities have contributed significantly to FCW waste reduction, many material flow problems are actually 'purchased' as packaging and products. Service industries such as hotels can make significant impacts by managing their supply chain relationships. The FCW illustrates efforts to influence supplier initiatives with respect to material flows. The resort hotel's kitchen, for example, has worked with a major supplier to replace the traditional waxed cardboard boxes in which meat is transported with reusable plastic totes. This diverts at least half of a ton of bulky waste from the landfill annually. The FCW's golf course has negotiated with suppliers to purchase bulk fertiliser, which is then directly filled into machines as needed. This system saves over 1,500 plastic bags that would otherwise go to landfill.

Products with recycled and low-impact content are purchased when possible. Most of the hotel resort's cleaning products, for example, are bought from a national supplier specialising in industrial cleaning products that are produced to meet high ecological standards. Furthermore, the FCW is working with its corporate purchasing department on several projects designed to reduce waste production. For example, the purchasing department surveyed all major FCW suppliers to identify opportunities for partnership and improvement in environmental practices. It was found that approximately half of the respondents did have environmental policies and programmes in place. Additionally, over 80 per cent of suppliers contributed ideas for improving their environmental practices as regards their dealings with FCW.

Conserving energy and water

Hotel resort operations are particularly resource intensive in terms of energy and water consumption. Energy and water use can place significant stress of natural environments and the financial bottom lines of hotel operations. In order to monitor its energy and water consumption FCW has contracted an outside company. The company provides data on these matters to the hotel's Energy Solution group thus allowing it to determine the extent of its progress towards its stated goals of reduced energy and water usage. The Energy Solution group, amongst other things, have been responsible for undertaking a full lighting audit, and are working on a three-phase retrofit to convert from incandescent to fluorescent lamps. Fluorescent lamps last longer and save energy (reducing consumption from 100 to approximately 28 watts per light). The financial advantages to be gained from this project are significant. It is expected that the payback period for various components of this project will range from 6 months to 2 years, depending on the project programme. Furthermore, the hotel also offers fluorescent lamps to employees at cost so as to increase staff awareness of energy savings.

Infrastructure initiatives to reduce water consumption include installing low-flow showers and toilets in all guest rooms. To reduce water on the golf course, FCW has also devised a stringent monitoring programme for its irrigation system. All water use is recorded and audited regularly. Additionally, maintenance staff irrigate only the dry areas that need attention, rather then watering the entire course on a regular basis.

Guests are also involved with conservation through FCW's sheet and towel change programme. Rather than changing guest sheets daily, longer-term guests are informed that their sheets will be changed every three days, unless they request otherwise. This programme resulted in CA$125,000 in energy savings in the first year. Furthermore, towels are only laundered when guests indicate that they would like to have them changed. The hotel resort estimates that 30 per cent of guests choose not to have towels washed everyday. These policies not only save water, energy, detergent, and transportation emissions, but also extend the life of the sheets and towels.

Conserving natural areas

To facilitate the implementation of sound environmental practices, it is advantageous to incorporate environmental objectives into the physical design and programming of tourism facilities. Design the operations at the FCW golf course illustrate this principle. The course's original design helped the facility to retain animal habitat and reduce maintenance costs. Of the 85 acre golf course expanse, 30 acres receive no maintenance at all; 50 acres are mowed regularly and are only fertilised once annually with a 70 per cent organic slow release formula. Less than 1 per cent of the course's turf is ever treated with chemical pesticides and fungicides. This only occurs when necessary to control weed or pest outbreaks. The development design ensured that healthy riparian zones were left bordering the three trout-breeding streams that flow through the golf course. Furthermore, many of the maintenance staff have been trained and certified as streamkeepers by the Pacific Streamkeepers Federation. They are responsible for the weekly monitoring of the number and species of fish that migrate through the creek, and pass this information along to the local municipality for their ongoing Monitoring Programme. Other conservation efforts supported by the hotel resort include educational talks and training about local bear populations, bird and tree species, as well as interpretative signage and pamphlets used communicate with guests and visitors.

Providing sustainable products

The FCW has been innovative in developing services that support sustainability principles. One manner in which sustainable services can be promoted is to obtain and communicate the importance of environmental certification to visitors and employees. The golf course, for example, has achieved and maintains 'Audubon Co-operative Sanctuary System' certification. This indicates that its operations meet high industry standards, as evaluated by an independent third party.

The FCW has also developed other unique services that are based on sound environmental principles. For instance, it has implemented a green meeting product called 'EcoMeet.' This package of environmental products is available to meeting and convention planners and their clients. It offers four optional components; eco-service, eco-cuisine, eco-accommodation and eco-programming. Each of these components meets between 12 to 20 specific criteria. For example, criteria for 'eco-cuisine' include using organic ingredients for meals. Other criteria include a mini-audit on meeting waste, biodegradable pens, environmental rooms, and activities with environmentally and socially responsible tour providers.

Social sustainability practices

The ideals of sustainable tourism extend beyond the protection and conservation of the ecological environment to ensuring the sustainability of the surrounding cultural and social environments. Ventures should be undertaken to maintain respectful, inclusive and capacity building relationships between residents, visitors, employees and other groups. The FCW engages in a various partnerships of this kind. It has implemented and continues to develop both community and employee programmes to strengthen the social fabric upon which its operations depend. An overview of these programmes follows:

> *Forming partnerships*: Active engagement in community life is a critical tool for strengthening relations among businesses and residents in tourism dependent regions. Involvement with local groups is an important step in achieving both environmental goals and the ethos of social sustainability. Partners working together towards attaining common goals may be more effective in achieving important objectives than might otherwise be possible. Such partnerships highlight the many inter dependencies that exist between the resort hotel and the broader social, environmental and economic issues confronting the Whistler community. They also illustrate examples where members are dedicated to working together in defining and achieving a common vision.
>
> The TNS partnership between the FCW and five other Whistler community groups is a good example of collaboration among local business, government and residents in support of community values. This strategic alliance has been critical in supporting the community's efforts at developing a more sustainable future. Similarly, FCW's participation in the Whistler

Fisheries Stewardship Group programme has strengthened the ability of that organisation to mitigate local stream degradation resulting from increased development at Whistler. A collective of the three local golf courses (including the FCW golf facility) called the 'Whistler Golf Sustainability Consortium' provides another example of how groups can operate move effectively as a team. The three organisations have crafted a common vision of what golf courses in Whistler might look like in an ideal future. They share resources, learning and purchasing power in order to reach their goals and vision.

- *Engaging volunteers*: Small communities tend to rely on a familiar circle of hard-working volunteers. To support such efforts, the FCW encourages wider involvement through grants to local volunteer groups. Five of these grants were awarded in 2000. The hotel also hosts an annual 'Volunteer Fair,' where local groups are invited to set up booths and promote their programme in order to engage new supporters. This fun event engages staff, schools, community members and even guests!
- *'Room with a View' programme:* In 1995, the Chateau Whistler formed an alliance with the British Columbia Children's Hospital in an effort to help sick children and demonstrate community support. The FCW provides opportunities for some of these patients to visit Whistler with their families or caregivers and stay for up to five free nights at the resort hotel. Through this FCW programme 30 to 40 families are accommodated at the resort hotel every year.
- *'Adopt a Shelter' programme*: The FCW has paired up with a nearby community women's shelter and offers support for this programme. At least one van-load of used furniture, drapery, bedding, kitchenware and other goods are donated on a weekly basis to the shelter. This initiatives is helping the shelter to continue to support women in need and assist them in establishing new homes after leaving the shelter. FCW's maintenance staff also visit the shelter frequently and perform odd repair jobs free of charge to help keep the building in good condition.

Supporting local products: Initiatives that support local talent and products contribute to both economic and social community sustainability. The FCW believes in recognising and building local capacity, and demonstrates this commitment in many ways. Much of the artwork found in the hotel resort has been produced by regional artists. The menus in the hotel resort's main restaurant are decorated with local wildflowers painted by a long-time Whistler resident. Many of the paintings found on the hotel's walls are images of local landscapes painted by a nearby Squeamish First Nations artist. Also many of the materials used in the construction of the hotel were locally manufactured or purchased. For example, the stone surrounding the hotel fireplaces came from a nearby quarry, and a local stonemason created the mantles. The FCW also purchases many of its seasonal food products from local suppliers supporting local growers both socially and financially. In addition, the hotel resort supports a weekly farmers' market in front of the hotel where local produce, crafts and other items are sold. This market supports the local economy and assists in creating a sense of community for both Whistler visitors and residents.

FCW Charity Foundation: A recent initiative which is fully volunteer-driven is the establishment of an official FCW Charity Foundation. The hotel resort's employees organise events and use other opportunities to raise funds that are then redistributed to local non-profit benefactors through the Foundation. For example, when a school group from the Vancouver Native Education Centre was hosted for a field trip, the cost of the entire day including lunch was sponsored by the Foundation. Additionally, several annual fund-raising events are organised, including a golf tournament and an evening concert. External donations to the Foundation are also encouraged.

Supporting employee living expenses: Housing and general living costs in resort communities are often high. The cost of living in Whistler is no exception. Finding affordable accommodation is a significant problem for both seasonal workers and more permanent residents, even though the Whistler municipality has taken various steps to help alleviate these pressures. In light of this problem, the FCW helps its employees by providing 240 staff with housing at rates that are significantly below market rates (at least 25% less). The hotel continually seeks new opportunities to provide for more staff. It acquired another house in 2001, thus offering studio and one-bedroom apartments to an additional 24 employees. Generally, the younger and more transient staff tend to live in these accommodations. However, to support those who live in nearby towns which are more affordable, the hotel resort offers a travel subsidy.

Building employee capacity: Employees are the heart of hotel operations and the FCW sets high standards in providing a safe and meaningful workplace. An employee's personal and professional growth is a priority at FCW. All new staff are greeted with a two and half day orientation. This emphasis on development continues. Training investments in 2000 totalled about CA$3 million, with 615 employees undertaking programmes. The hotel resort also has a progressive career development programme with a policy of internal promotion where possible. It also provides full funding for part-time external studies. These training programmes help to remove the traditional 'glass ceilings' often confronting local people wanting to advance in the tourism industry. They also help to build an empathetic and co-operative culture within the organisation.

Future Developments

Although the FCW's efforts towards more sustainable forms to tourism practice qualify them as a leading industry example, the organisation is continuing to strive for improvement. FCW plans to increase its efforts to create more sustainable operations by addressing challenges in the following areas.

Management systems

FCW needs to ensure that environmental and social objectives are prioritised and integrated into daily activities. Management and staff operate in a fast-paced, ever-changing environment, one in which employment turnover is endemic. Therefore, it is important that sustainability objectives are reflected in cultural values as well as operational and management systems. FCW intends to address these challenges by tying its environmental and social objectives to existing employee evaluation practices. FCW also intends to expand its measurement and reporting system to include environmental and social indicators. The importance of these additional metrics is highlighted by the Director of Operations' comment that 'we would do things quite differently if environmental and social objectives were measured as closely as financial objectives.'

Supply chain management

Through purchasing practices, the FCW has enormous opportunity to influence the sustainability of its own organisation along with those of its suppliers and service providers. By phasing out products, packaging and services that generate negative environmental impacts, the hotel reduces its need for internal programmes to deal with their consequences. In its efforts to address 'upstream' material flow problems, the FCW is focusing on supplier relationships. However, one of the many purchasing challenges it faces is that many of its products are purchased through corporate nation-wide contracts. In response to this, FCW plans to work very closely with its parent companies' regional and national purchasing departments in setting and achieving procurement goals that reflect FCW material flow reduction philosophies.

Community and Other Partnerships

As has been discussed previously, partnerships and collaboration allow groups to pool resources and attain goals that they might not be able to achieve individually. The FCW and other community businesses could further broaden community sustainability practices through the development of additional strategic partnerships. FCW could, for example, build on existing relationships with other organisations that promote and support sustainable practices. For example, the hotel resort might explore collaboration opportunities with regional non-profit organisations that promote environmentally responsible tourism. The FCW might also benefit from greater stakeholders input in its decision-making processes. Although many managers live in Whistler and are members of local groups, the hotel currently lacks programmes that involve wider stakeholders in planning policy review or decision processes.

Lessons Learned

As FCW has sought to progress its efforts in the area of sustainable tourism development, its management have learned a number of important lessons. Of these, perhaps five stand out as major 'signposts' for other tourism business seeking to travel this path.

(1) Take small, focused steps

The FCW has found that the best way to overcome the daunting nature of achieving sustainability ideals is to simply focus on principles and long-term goals, begin with small steps, and learn from these. A step-by-step approach builds the motivation, credibility and capacity that are needed to set and achieve new and future successes. Furthermore, early initiatives are also often those that have higher financial returns, which can then be invested into programmes that may be more challenging or have lower immediate returns.

(2) Measure outcomes

The FCW recognises the value of baselines, benchmarks and measurement. It is important to document material and energy flows in order to gauge levels of improvement over time. If there are no initial baselines or inaccurate benchmark measurements, it is not possible to track the benefits of initiatives. Without such measures, it is difficult to justify future action and resource allocations. Such monitoring is critical in gaining support for further projects and encouraging others to undertake similar initiatives.

(3) Staff involvement

The FCW has grown to appreciate the value of building staff understanding and ownership of programmes. The process by which an initiative is implemented, or a plan is designed, can be just as important as the actual initiative or the plan itself. Environmental and social sustainability ideals are operationalised differently throughout the organisation. As employees are the experts within their own operational areas, all staff must be involved for success. FCW strives to be clear in its communication and inclusive in its programme design so that affected staff understand the reasons behind initiatives and can be motivated to implement change.

(4) Communicate the organisation's 'story'

The FCW has learned that it is important to create a vision and a story that everybody understands, talks about and contributes to. Such a story-line about events and successes builds excitement and momentum. It also allows individuals to communicate these events to other groups. FCW has recently begun to be more purposeful in sharing its story with staff in presentations and daily conversation. Furthermore, the hotel resort has also found that it is helpful to initiate projects that are highly visible and affect many employees, as these clearly communicate cultural values and management commitment.

(5) Leadership

The FCW is committed to a leadership role in achieving sustainability concepts and goals. Their approach to achieving more sustainable operations presents a useful learning tool for others in the Resort Municipality of Whistler and in the tourism industry. The hotel resort has set the stage for a new operational model. It now faces the challenge of broadening its circle of influence and support, and further entrenching sustainability values into its organisational culture and systems. If it is to be successful in this regard it needs to foster creativity and learning as regards sustainable development, and continue to push beyond the boundaries of its existing activities.

Conclusion

FCW has sought to engage with the principles and concepts associated with sustainable tourism development in a strategic fashion. In doing so it has sought to integrate its various dimensions into its own organisational fabric, as well as that of the businesses and community with which it interacts. Also, it has embraced a broad view of sustainable development, extending beyond protection and conservation of the ecological environment to also include its surrounding cultural and social environments.

As FCW has engaged with the concept of sustainable development over the past ten years, it has learned a number of key lessons, central amongst which are: the need to adopt a step-by-step approach guided by defined principles and long-term goals; the importance of measuring outcomes; the significance of staff involvement in programmes and activities; the value of creating a vision and a story around the organisation's sustainable development activities; and the significance of leadership in both the successful introduction of a sustainability programme, and in its broader acceptance by other businesses and the community.

12

Wildlife Conservation, Tourism and the Private Sector

The Australian environment has changed markedly since the arrival of the early European settlements, due mostly to land clearance for agriculture, pasture creation, housing and industry. Additionally, feral animals and introduced plants have invaded vast areas, significantly degrading ecosystems as they have spread across the country. The outcome of these developments has been to place Australia's rich biodiversity under threat. In the first *State of the Environment* report commissioned by the Federal government, large numbers of mammal (29 %), bird (20 %), reptile (7 %), fish (13 %), and amphibian (15 %) species were identified as being either extinct, endangered or vulnerable. As regards plant species, 16 per cent of Australia's wild plant species are now estimated to have originated from overseas. Additionally, 5 per cent of native plants have been identified as being endangered or vulnerable. These worrying trends have been in evidence in Australia for many years, and served to provide Dr. John Wamsley with the rationale for the establishment of Earth Sanctuaries Propriety Limited in 1988, and later (1993) Earth Sanctuaries Limited.

The case study seeks to examine the central role of tourism in the business strategy of Earth Sanctuaries Limited (ESL), Australia's first publicly listed company with the stated primary goal of conserving wildlife, and the reasons why the future of this organisation is now in doubt. The case study begins by giving a brief overview of the development of ESL from a single sanctuary to the present; ESL currently operates ten such areas. It then examines ESL's mission, objectives and business strategy and overviews its conservation outcomes to date. The final part of this case study discusses key causal factors that have led to the present situation where ESL's future, at least in its current form, is under immediate threat. Central amongst these factors, it is argued here, is the balance the organisation has struck between its business mission of conservation and its need as a publicly listed company to generate a return to its shareholders, primarily from tourism related services.

Origins and Development

In 1969 Dr. John Wamsley purchased a 14-hectare property in the Adelaide Hills, South Australia, that he named Warrawong. This property had previously been used as a dairy farm and was devoid of native vegetation. Wishing to repair the damage from 100 years of intensive farming and restore the area's flora and fauna, Dr. Wamsley embarked on an extensive re-vegetation programme. By 1980 he had been successful in establishing over 50,000 native plants on the property, but found that native birds and animals attracted back by maturing vegetation were falling prey to cats and foxes. To overcome this problem he built a vermin-proof fence around his land, with the result that the bird and animal population within the compound rose sharply. At this time, he also began to introduce into Warrawong rare and endangered mammal species which, in the absence of predators, also thrived. These animals included the Short-nosed Bandicoot, Rufus Bettong and Red Necked Wallaby.

The success Wamsley experienced at Warrawong caused him to think in terms of creating similar fenced environments at other locations, and of how he could fund a network of such reserves. He opened Warrawong to the public in 1985, seeking to determine if tourism could be used to underpin his efforts. At this property he: conducted morning and afternoon guided walks; built a number of self-contained tents; developed a restaurant and souvenir store; and catered for smallscale conferences and weddings. He was sufficiently satisfied with the Warrawong experiment to form the view that tourism could play a significant role in supporting an expanded organisation, the core business of which was conservation.

With the intention of pursuing this objective, Wamsley established Earth Sanctuaries Propriety Limited in 1988. Through this company he began developing a number of sanctuaries, employing a staged development process based in large measure on the one he had used at Warrawong. This process, in essence, involved: selecting a habitat zone in which to establish a sanctuary; identifying the least degraded, most representative area within the identified zone; constructing a fenced compound around all, or part of, the site; eradicating feral animals; reintroducing (as required) animals that once lived in the area; commencing a programme of habitat re-vegetation (as required); developing an interpretation plan in order to protect the site from the impact of visitors and to facilitate their understanding of it; and the development of tourism infrastructure and supporting visitor management systems. By the end of 2001 ESL was operating ten sanctuaries, four of which had moved through these stages of the point where they had been opened to the public.

Over a 12-year period from 1988, ESL raised AU$21.1 million to support its mission. ESL's capital-raising efforts were assisted in large measure by its founder's decision to change the structure of the business from a private company to that of a public company (Earth Sanctuaries Limited) in 1993, and the later listing of this company in 2000 on the Australian Stock Exchange. By the end of 2001 ESL's capital base had allowed it to establish nine sanctuaries. Additionally, it was acting on behalf of a US based company to manage a tenth sanctuary. These areas in total covered approximately 90,000 hectares of which some 9,500 were feral fenced.

ESL's growth from a single to a multi-site business is reflected in its overall operational and business practices. ESL's business structure had evolved from essentially that of a 'sole trader' to that of a public company, whose board, at the end of 2001, processed a strong business, as opposed to conservation, background. Board members at this time included three chartered accountants, two solicitors and one business economist. Also in place at this time was a professional management team comprising a CEO, five sanctuary managers, and one Wildlife Officer. Additionally, ESL had developed substantial expertise in raising funds from capital markets to fuel its growth. Indeed, ESL had seemingly addressed many of the weaknesses identified by McKercher (1998) of small nature based tourism enterprises. These included: reliance on a small management team; strong owner influence; few specialist staff; performance of a variety of roles by management; and a limited ability to attract finance.

Mission, Objectives and Business Strategy

ESL's state mission is to conserve Australia's unique biodiversity by creating at least one sanctuary in each of its 80 major habitat zones. Whilst some of ESL's corporate objectives reflect its concern to operate successfully as a business, most reflect this mission specifically:

- conserving Australia's flora and fauna within a commercial environment;
- developing sanctuaries within the major habitat zones in Australia;
- providing a programme of interpretation and education at each sanctuary;
- operating each sanctuary in a sustainable way; and
- providing assistance, by way of a constancy service, to landholders seeking to conserve biodiversity on their land.

Tourism has been significant factor in ESL's strategic thinking since the company's formation. Reflective of this has been the more than doubling of tourism specific revenue from approximately AU$600,000 in 1994 to AU$1.4 million in 2000 (or approximately 75% of ESL's total revenue). Other revenue sources include: a consultancy service providing advice on feral animal eradication, native animal management and feral proof fencing; feral animal proof fence construction; and management services for private sanctuaries. However, ESL has not been able to fund its growth from these activities. Instead it has relied largely on its capital raising activities for this purpose. In this regard recent years have seen ESL operate at a cash deficit of AU$2.5 million per annum, a situation which ESL acknowledges cannot be sustained.

Recognising the need to refocus ESL's business strategy in order to address its major cash flow problem, the ESL board, under the leadership of its newly appointed chairman Dr. Don Stammer (a business economist), made the decision in 1999 to limit land purchases and most of its property development activities to areas in close proximity to selected major population centres on Australia's east coast (*i.e.*, Melbourne, Sydney and Canberra) for a five-year period. This decision was made in the express purpose of significantly growing tourism revenue to the point where a cash surplus would result, allowing ESL to fund future growth from this source. To progress this strategy ESL listed on the Australia Stock Exchange in 2000. This listing was successful in raising AU$12.3 million.

Money raised from ESL's float was largely allocated to the development of an area 50 minutes driving time from the centre of Melbourne which ESL had previously purchased for AU$5.5 million. This site is known as Little River Sanctuary. According to a feasibility study conducted by the consulting firm KPMG the site was projected to generate a cash surplus after three years, and by 2000, a profit of AU$3.049 million per annum based on an estimated 100,000 visitors. Such projections were not unrealistic given the performance of similar reserves in the state of Victoria that provide opportunities to view rare Australian wildlife. For example, a Penguin reserve (Phillip Island Nature Reserve), located 1.5 hours driving time from Melbourne, attracts, over 5,00,000 visitors annually. It should also be noted that the business climate in which Little River would have opened was predicted to have been a favourable one from a tourism perspective. The Tourism Forecasting Council of Australia (2001) anticipated average growth rates of 7.8 per cent per annum in inbound tourism and 1.9 per cent per annum in domestic tourism, for the ensuing ten years.

Profit from the Little River Sanctuary was to be directed by ESL into the development of two recently purchased east-coast sanctuary sites, specifically Blue Mountains (approximately 2.75 hours driving time from Sydney) and Mullawollen (1.5 hours drive north of the nations capital, Cenberra). Towards the end of ESL's first five-year east-coast development plan it also intended, depending on profit performance to establish further sanctuaries, this time in Queensland, near the large population centres of Brisbane and the Gold Coast.

Conservation Outcomes

According to ESL's 2001 Annual Report, its land heirings contain populations of 15 species of endangered, threatened or rare animals that collectively total 2,285 individuals. These animals include: Southern Brown Bandicoot, Brush Tailed Bettong, Rufous Bettong, Yellow Footed Rock Wallaby, Bilby, Platypus, Eastern Quoll, Bridled Nantail Wallaby, Stick Nest Rats, Hairy-nosed Wombats and Numbats. Additionally, significant regeneration of native plant species has occurred, particularly inside fenced areas, at some sanctuary sites. For example, Wamsley estimates that after fencing a large area of Yookamurra, and removing rabbits and goats, an additional six million plants have germinated and survived.

Regular translocation of small numbers of animals between sanctuaries has been occurring for some years in order to minimise problems of inbreeding and to reintroduce species to areas where they have long since vanished. Additionally, animals are regularly exchanged with Australian Zoos and National Parks and Wildlife Services in order to manage genetic diversity. ESL has also been successful in obtaining breeding stock of several rare, endangered or threatened animals from national park agencies, such as the Rufous Hare Wallaby (Queensland National Parks and Wildlife Service) and the Western Bilby (Northern Territory Parks and Wildlife Commission).

ESL can be said to have played a significant role in educating not only visitors to its sanctuaries on aspects of Australia's native fauna and flora and the difficulties they face, but the broader community as well. As regards the latter, ESL has attracted significant media coverage in Australia and overseas (*e.g.*, *Life Magazine*), assisted by the many (20) tourism-related awards it has won since 1988, including a prestigious Conde Nast Traveller's Choice Award in the category of Ecotourism. Wamsley's personal efforts, such as the wearing of a cat skin hat to public functions, have also been particularly successful in drawing public attention to ESL and its mission.

Causal Factors Threatening ESL's Future

Investor perspectives and financial performance

The financial market's view of ESL, and its current strategic direction, has been somewhat contradictory up until very recently. A number of stockbroking firms, such as Falkiners Stockbroking Limited and Findlay and Co. Limited, viewed ESL as a sound long-term investment, with the latter recently stating:

> Earth Sanctuaries Limited is an excellent investment for those wishing to make a contribution to the conservation of Australia's wildlife, while also investing in the longer term. A more ethical investment would be difficult to find, and as shown in the following cash flow analysis, the wilderness sanctuaries should be self-sustaining within a five year period. The share price is likely to be driven by a continuing strong appetite for 'feel good' ethical investments that also provide the real prospect for commercial returns.

Other stockbroking firms viewed ESL, in a less positive light. The stock broking firm Ethical Investment Services, for example, advised its clients not to invest in Earth Sanctuaries, and suggested to those that did to 'assume your investment is more of a donation for the next few years.' Another firm, AMP Henderson Global Investors, did not include ESL shares as part of its Sustainable Future Fund, as it did not achieve the fund's financial objectives. Given that ESL's dividends were of a nominal nature, and that no dividends at all were paid in 2001, such views are understandable. Indeed, ESL's lack of short- to medium-term returns is likely to have been central in its share price falling from AU$2.50 when it first listed in 2000 to AU$1.60 a few months later.

Before resigning in January 2002, ESL's then chairman noted that it was likely to be the case that many of ESL's investors were more concerned with the idea embodied in the Earth Sanctuary concept than with profit. Supporting this view is the fact that a significant percentage of investors (10% in 2000) donated their dividends back to ESL, while still others indicated their intent to bequeath their shares to the company. The 'well' of such investors is, however, not fathomless as ESL has discovered. Requiring a further AU$7 million to complete its Little River Sanctuary, ESL has been unable to raise any additional funds via the share market. Without this additional equity, and the cash flow that a completed Little River Sanctuary would generate, ESL's future, at least in its current form, is now very much in doubt.

Unable to raise additional equity, and with the real potential of facing future cash flow difficulties, ESL made its situation known to the stock market in January 2002 resulting in its share price falling rapidly to 16 cents per share, down from a listing price of AU$2.50 18 months earlier. At the time of writing ESL had appointed a consultancy firm, Challenger Corporate Finance, to assist it in restructuring its operations. As part of this process expressions of interest have been sought for the purchase of all ESL assets. The immediate past chairman of ESL summed up the situation that led to the difficult financial position ESL now faces by noting that 'had the 7000 shareholders got a good feeling in both their heart and their pocket, it would have been easier . . . to raise money on the stock exchange.'

Nature of Core Assets

A key factor influencing ESL's poor share price performance is the nature of its core assets. Unlike, for example, traditional wildlife parks, which tend to showcase animals for profit, ESL's conservation focus meant that it spent considerable money, time and energy seeking to develop assets in the form of rare, endangered or threatened species, which presently cannot be sold and, as such, have no market value. This situation was compounded, until recently, by Australian Accounting Standard AASB 1010 that stated that '. . . the revaluation of a class of non-current assets shall be its recoverable amount.' This approach to valuing assets meant that ESL was precluded from valuing its natural resources in any way other than that which would be able to be obtained from their sale on the open market. As both the commonwealth and state governments in Australia have extensive legislation dealing with the protection of native fauna and flora and associated trade in, and property rights to, native species, ESL's ability to do this, and therefore benefit financially from its core activity of conservation, was extremely limited. This situation, to some extent, on the 1st of July, 1998 when Accounting Standard AASB 1037, which covers self-generating and regenerating assets, was introduced. This standard applied to all companies from the financial years ended 30th June, 2001. Essentially, this changed ruling allowed ESL to place a value on its fauna and record this value on its balance sheet.

The approach which ESL decided to employ to value its fauna assets under AASB 1037 was to value them using the cost of re-establishing species' populations and associated translocation costs. Using this approach, the following valuations were made in 2001:

- *Threatened species*—species requires some form of conserva-tion due to its vulnerability—AU$1500 per animal;
- *Rare species*—species numbers have declined to the point where it is likely to move into the endangered category in the near future if causal factors continue— AU$3000 per animal; and
- *Endangered species*—the species is in danger of extinction—AU$6000 per animal.

Based on these values, the net market value of animals on ESL land in 2001 was calculated to be AU$412,000. This calculation was made based on a species census, the validity of which was determined by an external consultant from the University of Adelaide. While such figures better reflect the company's value, they do not enhance borrowing power, nor do they influence dividend growth significantly, as ESL cannot, as noted previously, sell its animal assets under present government regulations.

Business Strategy

Unlike public sector conservation organisations, such as national park agencies, ESL's future, given its private sector nature, is not underwritten by the public purse. Indeed, as Gray (2002) points out, the reason why most protected areas are public goods in the first place is that the private sector cannot extract a profit from their operation after paying for maintenance and general upkeep. Compounding this problem is the observation that a similar product to that offered by ESL to consumers is available free or at a low cost from national parks.

Another difficulty faced by ESL is the cost of moving an area of land through the stages noted previously before it could be opened to the public. In the case of the Little River Sanctuary; for example, AU$6 million had been spent on land purchase, fencing, water and power infrastructure, architect fees and habitat restoration before development was suspended.

Given restrictions on the trade in wildlife, ESL's decision to use tourism as its main cash flow vehicle could reasonably be seen as a sound business strategy. It's early decisions, however, to purchase land in locations remote from major population centres (*i.e.*, Yookamurra, Scotia, Tiparra, Dakalanta, and Buckaringa sanctuaries), and therefore potential tourist markets, appears to have been guided more by conservation than tourism considerations. This observation has been made by several observers of ESL's current situation, including Barry Cohen, a former Federal Environment Minister, and himself a wildlife sanctuary operator Cohen believes that most of ESL's sanctuaries were simply too far from major tourist markets to generate adequate revenue from visitation. Hamilton of the think-tank The Australia Institute, also makes this point adding that such location decisions appear to be the outcome of confusing environmental goals with commercial goals.

ESL's east-coast strategy arguably held out significant potential for generating the revenue necessary to improve its cash flow situation and hence its stock exchange performance, but it was not without risk. ESL through this strategy was moving into a market place where it was likely to confront significant competition from established wildlife park operators with long standing links with the tourism industry, particularly tour operators. Little River Sanctuary, for example, would have been one of five private wildlife parks/reserves within 1.5 hours by road from Melbourne, although it would have been amongst the closest of these. In the case of Sydney, there are six established wildlife parks/reserves, all significantly closer (by 1 hour or more by road) to the Central Business District (CBD) than the two sanctuary sites (Blue Mountains and Mullawollen) ESL had purchased for later development. The issue of location is particularly significant when the time and budgetary constraints that many tourists operate under are taken into account. Related to this are the restrictions that location (and associated travelling time) can place on the capacity of day tour operators based in, or near, CBD locations to package product such as that of ESL's.

While competition was likely to have been a factor in ESL's successful entry into east-coast markets, the uniqueness of the ESL product, with visitors being able to experience rare, threatened and endangered wildlife in a natural setting, may well have provided it with a significant marketing edge. This 'edge,' however, was unlikely to go unchallenged in the medium-to-long-term. Already one sanctuary, Calga Springs, 1 hours drive north of Sydney, had employed a similar sanctuary development model to that used by ESL. This fully feral free reserve opened to the public in March 2001.

The success of ESL's east-coast strategy is also likely to have been affected by the need to 'bleed' off some of the profits it might have generated to maintain its existing sanctuaries, most of which were not open to the public. While ESL had begun to address this issue by placing some 'non-performing' sanctuaries up for sale in 2000 and 2001, such efforts may have been perceived by the market as too little and too late.

ESL's business strategy essentially involved the ownership of all its sanctuary sites, the exception being Hansen Bay on Kangaroo Island that it managed under contract. This being the case its growth was limited by its ability to attract new capital through the sale of shares, or its capacity to generate a profit from its operations, some of which could then be used for reinvestment purposes. A possible way around this limitation which was not explored by ESL is the business strategy of franchising. There would have been a number of potential benefits available to ESL through the employment of such an approach, including the ability to expand the number of its sites at a significantly faster rate than that which otherwise would be the case, and at minimum business risk. However, to engage in franchising, ESL would have needed to refine its business, animal management and visitor servicing systems to the point where they could easily be duplicated, with appropriate assistance from ESL, at new locations. Given that in New South Wales alone, an area one-third the size of the national park estate (approximately 5,00,000 hectares) is gazetted as private wildlife refuges, the alternative of franchising may still be worth considering by a restructured ESL.

Conclusion

The conservation process is generally viewed as one that produces public rather than private benefits. ESL has sought to challenge this assumption with a business model that is dependent largely on tourism and that seeks to produce both conservation outcomes and financial returns to shareholders. The idea embodied in ESL has inspired investors to support its growth from a single 'outlet' operation in 1988 to an AU$20 million dollar-plus enterprise with ten locations some 12 years later. The 'well' of investors willing to support ESL in the absence of short- to medium-term financial returns would appear, however, to have been exhausted. ESL now finds itself in the position of not being able to implement its current five-year strategy of developing sanctuaries near east-coast population centres in order to grow its tourism revenue base, and of needing to restructure its operations dramatically simply to survive. This restructuring could well see ESL revert to a one or two sanctuary operation in the absence of a 'white knight' with a willingness to provide the AU$7 million or more required to allow it to continue its present strategy.

The central problem in ESL's case appears to have been the balance which it originally struck between its conservation and revenue generation goals and which were finally judged by the market place to be unacceptable. While ESL's assertion that tourism would eventually develop to the point where meaningful returns would be paid to shareholders might well have proven true in the longer term, the market was not willing to wait. ESL's initial strategy of locating sanctuaries in areas of high conservation value, but removed from major population centres, compounded the problem of generating acceptable returns from tourism. Its revised east-coast strategy, from the market's perspective, might also have been seen as having some level of risk associated with it given that meaningful levels of competition were present on the east coast from both private sector wildlife parks and national park services.

As ESL seeks to chart a revised course in order to shore up its short-term future, certain key lessons would appear evident. Given the severely constrained capacity of ESL to engage in the sale of endangered, rare or threatened wildlife, ESL's conservation agenda needed to be circumscribed by its capacity to generate revenue, primarily from tourism. This being the case, ESL's ultimate goal of developing sanctuaries in all major habitat zones in Australia, while highly commendable, was unlikely to be achievable through a reliance on tourism. The visitation levels required to support the ESL sanctuary development process are realistically available only at certain locations. Acknowledgement of this can be found in ESL's somewhat belated decision to focus its attention on the development of east-coast sites from 1999, a decision which might reflect the change in its board at this time.

Whatever view is taken in ESL's current plight, it still must be acknowledged that this enterprise was the first with the stated goal of conservation to list on the Australian Stock Exchange, and to raise substantial funds by so doing. If ESL is successful in its restructuring efforts, the lessons it has learnt to date will likely see it strike a more pragmatic balance between conservation and the need for revenue, particularly from tourism. Such a balance will probably result in a revised, and less grand mission for the organisation, particularly if it again seeks to own and operate its sanctuaries. As regards this last point, the possibility of franchising sanctuaries, a common business growth strategy in many sectors of the tourism industry, may offer ESL some prospect for longer-term growth. Given the large amount of private land already gazetted as wildlife refuges in states such as NSW, there may indeed be many John Wamsleys ready and willing to take up the conservation challenge under ESL's and in a commercially responsible way.

Index